THUNDER IN THE VALLEY

Doug and Evelyn Knapp
with Robert O'Brien
Foreword by Owen Cooper

Broadman Press
Nashville, Tennessee

© Copyright 1986 ● Broadman Press
All Rights Reserved
4263-42
ISBN: 0-8054-6342-9
Dewey Decimal Classification: 266.092
Subject Headings: KNAPP, DOUGLAS // KNAPP, EVELYN //
MISSIONS - TANZANIA
Library of Congress Catalog Number: 86-17147
Printed in the United States of America

Library of Congress Cataloging-in-Publication Data

Knapp, Doug, 1927-
   Thunder in the valley.

   1. Knapp, Doug, 1927-   . 2. Knapp, Evelyn,
1930-   . 3. Missionaries—Tanzania—Biography.
4. Missionaries—United States—Biography. 5. Baptists—
Missions—Tanzania. I. Knapp, Evelyn, 1930-
II. O'Brien, Robert, 1939-   . III. Title.
BV3625.T4K62 1986   266′.6132′0922 [B]   86-17147
ISBN 0-8054-6342-9 (pbk.)

Dedication

Dedicated to Suzanne, Walter, Richard, Edson, Joylene, Leslie, Douglas, Simon, Luke, Crystal, and other missionary kids (MKs), who give so much of themselves while their parents follow God's call to the most remote corners of the world.

MAP BY NANCY WOGSLAND

Foreword

by Owen Cooper

"Farm Boy Makes Good."

"Farm Boy Achieves Outstanding Success."

Headlines like that have attracted my attention for the past half-century, as I have read of those born on the farm who have attained high places of leadership in our society. I have personally known young men who started with "nothing" and, through untiring effort and countless hours of labor, have built large and successful farming operations.

Others farm boys I've known have launched extensive, privately-owned ventures in the agribusiness, some growing into multi-billion dollar operations. Others have ascended the ladder of success to its top rungs in law, medicine, banking, insurance, transportation, manufacturing, merchandising, and other enterprises.

Then, I met another farm boy, Doug Knapp, whose remarkable career fills the pages of this exciting, fascinating book, *Thunder in the Valley*.

He grew up on a small farm in Florida where his folks raised commercial flowers. *Intensive agricul-*

ture, they called it. He planted seed and waited until the warmth of God-given sunshine, the moisture of God-provided rain, and the food of God-created plant nutrients combined to germinate the seed, produce the plants, and then crown them with beautiful flowers.

Doug Knapp experienced God's endless miracle of planting and harvesting as he grew up and then studied about it in agricultural degree programs in college and graduate school.

Then the Lord touched the lives of Doug and his wife, Evelyn, in an unusual manner, calling them to get off the corporate ladder of agribusiness, to leave the challenging life of an agriculturist in the United States, and to move to a remote area of Africa as missionaries.

God wanted Doug and Evelyn, dedicated laypersons, to use their knowledge of farming to feed the hungry, to improve the economic life of a whole tribe of people, and to demonstrate their commitment to Him by giving a word of witness to those who had never heard of Jesus Christ. They have demonstrated through a life of loving service that genuine joy comes from faith and satisfaction, from seeing people accept Christ.

Thunder in the Valley chronicles the amazing results springing from their willingness to answer the call and go to Tanzania, where they have fed the hungry and laid the groundwork over the past two decades for a spiritual breakthrough which will have an enduring impact on the history of African missions.

Jesus drew heavily from agriculture in His teachings and parables because His listeners understood sowing and reaping. Agricultural missionaries, such as the Knapps, direct their work toward people who are close to nature. Because they deal with those people in terms they can understand, such as Jesus did, they enhance the possibility of a response.

Agricultural missionaries know that if a person is hungry, Jesus Christ, the Bread of Life, is more palatable when He is served with bread from grain. They know that when a person is thirsty, Jesus Christ, the Living Water, is more acceptable when He is offered along with germ-free, cool water. They know that a Heavenly Home can be better understood and more eagerly sought when a family's economic condition has improved to the point that their own home is more than a hovel and has become a place of comfort and security.

One of the problems facing agricultural missionaries is the high cost of establishing their work. They have a long shopping list beyond the needs of a preacher missionary, when you consider the need for land, buildings, fencing, livestock pens, facilities for chickens, hutches for rabbits, and other needs related to animal husbandry. Fuel, seed, fertilizer, insecticides, farm implements, machinery, and a host of other supplies are needed. Supplies are available sometimes on a donated basis from farmers in the United States, but the cost of moving them to mission areas is substantial.

I became involved with an organization known as Agricultural Missions Fellowship (AMF), through which farmers and agribusiness people worked together to provide supplemental help for agricultural missionaries. That was especially valuable when Southern Baptist world hunger contributions were small. But now that the Southern Baptist Foreign Mission Board has substantial funds for hunger relief and food production on the mission field, AMF has shifted more toward providing volunteers and technical assistance than in providing financial assistance.

I came to hear of Doug Knapp and to know him through AMF. Doug discovered the soil in Tanzania's Kyela District was especially adapted to pineapples, not the small ones grown in many areas but the large, sweet, juicy ones like those in Hawaii. He began experimenting with pineapples and the acreage began to multiply. The question arose about what to do with the pineapples, which are highly perishable. The long, bumpy, winding road to Dar es Salaam forbade the economical transportation to that area.

The possibility of a canning factory was discussed, and AMF entered the discussion. The proposed factory never developed for a variety of reasons, but the relationship continued with Doug, the former assistant county agent from Dade County (Miami), Florida, who was using modern agricultural techniques to increase food production and cash crops of the Nyakyusa tribe in Southwestern Tanzania.

After I met the Knapps, I became impressed with their unique work and the unusual response of the people to them. I learned what I could about them;

I read what was available about them; I prayed for them; my excitement about their work accelerated.

Before the Knapps came home in 1984-85 on a year's furlough, Baptist Press news service circulated the exciting story of the results of an earlier crusade conducted in their area by the Knapps and two teams of volunteers from the United States.

Generally, the teams were made up of about 40 percent pastors and 60 percent laypersons. The truth of the matter is that the eager ears of the Africans couldn't tell whether the Good News they heard came from the lips of pastor or layperson. Both came with the same message. Under the influence of the Holy Spirit, 7,505 Africans professed faith in Jesus Christ because of the message, not because of the messenger.

In 1984, Doug spoke on the program at the annual meeting of the Agricultural Missions Fellowship. The more I heard about his thrilling ministry, which produced nearly 34,000 baptisms and nearly 200 churches between 1978 and mid-1986 alone, the more I wanted to be sure Southern Baptists, and our fellow evangelicals, had the opportunity to read about it in expanded form—even a book.

I'm not a writer, but I know a good story when I hear one. With the idea of securing material that could be used in a book, my wife, Beth, and I met Doug and Evelyn in Destin, Florida. For three days, I taped their voices as they told their story, related their experiences, and revealed their dreams for the future. It resulted in a transcript of 375 typewritten pages.

During the discussion, Doug and Evelyn mentioned that Robert O'Brien (overseas news coordinator and senior communications consultant for the Foreign Mission Board) might agree to prepare a manuscript. Robert, who has lived in Africa and traveled widely there, has been to the area where the Knapps work and has first-hand knowledge of the situation there, as well as the work throughout Tanzania.

As time unfolded, Robert accepted the responsibility and scheduled a trip to Tanzania to coincide with the 1985 crusade, which once again would be led by volunteer pastors and laypersons. I gave him a copy of the transcript of my interviews, which he assured me was valuable. But most of his material came from the lips of Doug and Evelyn, as Robert provided a listening ear and activated tape recorder, and from his background knowledge of their work.

As I read the result of their collaboration, *Thunder in the Valley,* I had a new vision of the "farm boy who made good."

Forgotten was the vision of one who owned vast acreage and great productive capacity; forgotten was the image of one whose success was measured by a plush corporate office and a nine-figure balance sheet; forgotten was one whose vocation had given him financial security and professional acclaim.

Paramount in my mind was one whose commitment led him to forsake the opportunity to develop a large, personally-owned farming operation, whose call led him away from the corporate office and the paneled directors' room, and whose commission was to "go and share," not "stay and acquire."

The more I thought of this, the more it became apparent to me that the names of Doug Knapp and his helpmate, Evelyn, were fittingly at the top of my list of successful farm people, when judged by any standard related to human and spiritual values.

Several conclusions have reached out to grab me as I have kept up with the careers of Doug and Evelyn, interviewed them in minute detail, and read the manuscript prepared by Robert O'Brien. Without comment, I list them as follows:

1. *God has a call for everyone.* The call may come late in life. The call generally comes when one places himself/herself in a position and under the circumstances to listen.

2. *God has means of preparing us to fulfil the responsibilities inherent in His call, even though we may not be aware of the call during the period of preparation.*

3. *God can use all kinds of people in accomplishing His plan for this world. He can use pastors, educators, musicians, doctors, nurses, housewives, accountants, veterinarians, teachers, evangelists, the ordained, the unordained, and even agriculturalists.*

4. *Patience, commitment and love are all ingredients in ascertaining God's will and fulfilling His purpose through our lives—and the greatest of these is love.*

5. *Planned, long-range, systematic programs for*

evangelism are successful, whether in this country or abroad.

6. The first major effort in evangelism among those of non-Christian background is establishing credibility with the people and creating confidence in the missionary and trust in his objectives.

7. The use of volunteers (pastors, church staff members, laypersons) can pay off abundantly.

8. Prayer has a major part in undergirding crusades and in invoking the power of the Holy Spirit in evangelism.

9. The results of training and discipling the converts before baptizing them demonstrates the validity of such a procedure.

10. The establishment of a church within walking distance of each person in the district makes the Word of God available to all.

11. The use of national pastors and the training of these pastors and national evangelists have been essential ingredients in church growth and expansion.

12. The organization of churches into associations and the involvement of many people in evangelism, missions, youth work, and other activities has included not only the leaders but many church members in spreading the gospel.

13. God can use people of all ages. When Doug and Evelyn Knapp were ready to go to the field, they were eligible only because the Foreign Mission Board had increased the age limit. God can use the young, the middle-aged, and the old. It isn't how old you are, but how committed you are.

In an insightful way, Robert O'Brien has caught the commitment, the character, and the spirit of Doug and Evelyn Knapp. You will enjoy reading about these two dynamic people. The excitement of their lives is contagious, and as I read the manuscript, it increased my interest to a great commitment of mission involvement and being more involved in supporting mission programs, so that unknown "Doug and Evelyn Knapps" may be challenged to a mission career, called to mission service, and sent to mission lands.

Doug and Evelyn Knapp are modest and humble people. They are not too proud to make their home in a converted barn; they are not so conscious of creature comforts that they seek the cool altitudes of the plateau rather than the hot and humid climate in the river bottom; they are willing to live approximately fifty miles down sometimes impassable road from other missionaries so they can better identify with the nationals among whom they work; they are willing to work so the product of their hands can be an instrument to change the lives of those to whom they witness; they are willing to love first so they will become loved later; they are willing to serve so their service will become a living testimony; they are willing to give, not calculating that in giving they will receive overflowing blessing; and they are willing to share so, in sharing, they will reap an abundant harvest.

During one of his visits to Mississippi, Doug Knapp spoke to the weekly chapel service held at the Baptist Building in Jackson, Mississippi. A few days later,

I was visiting with Dr. Earl Kelly, executive secretary of the Mississippi Baptist Convention Board.

We commented about Doug's work and his visit, and Dr. Kelly referred to Doug as "Mr. Humility." A suitable description of a truly humble man.

Owen Cooper
Yazoo City, Mississippi

Contents

Praise Leaps

The hippos were leaping today, Lord,
Leaping,
Like frisky horses or calves,
Bounding out of the water.

The crocodiles slithered along
With only their eyes to give
Their presence away.

The egrets flapped in unison
As they went to roost.

The sky was a gray-pink washboard
With a mound of gray clothes
Waiting to be washed on it.

The spoonbills hurried along,
Scooping dessert before darkness
Ended their meal.

The elephants wanted a quick bath
Before their dinner.

The bee eaters, en masse, swept out
Of their high rise, cliff apartments.

And I could only watch in awe
As each creation seemed to be
Praising You, Lord,
Just by doing what You created it to do.

—Suzanne Knapp Groce

1
Drop by Drop

Simoni Mwambobe, his lean muscles rippling under his plaid, open-collared shirt, strode vigorously ahead of our small *safari*, every step showing his excitement.

"Bwana Nepu, Bwana Nepu, the river's up ahead," he called through the underbrush. "We'll soon be there."

Simoni's excitement affected us all. Evelyn's eyes met mine with emotion. We both realized this was another milestone in more than twenty years as bush missionaries in beautiful but remote southwestern Tanzania.

Our work among the Nyakyusa people of the lush, tropical Kyela (Key-AY-lah) District was truly going international, and Simoni might well qualify as the first "foreign missionary" for Tanzania Baptists. Soon we would cross the Songwe River into the country of Malawi to capitalize on his efforts.

Simoni, a young man with a quick mind and an infectious laugh, had come home to the Kyela District after losing an eye in a South African gold mine.

He eventually accepted Jesus Christ and became a pastor.

His church grew to eight-hundred members, huge by local standards, and he began to develop other churches. Eventually, he became one of six successful pastors we chose to help implement a master plan to evangelize the quarter-of-a-million people in the district.

Hot African sunlight glinted up ahead on the river and on the smiling ebony faces of the Nyakyusa men waiting eagerly at the bend of the river to help us clamber into a rough dugout canoe for the short trip to the Malawi side.

Our steps quickened in anticipation, and soon we stood at the edge of the chocolate-tinged water. The Songwe isn't a big river, only about eighty feet across, perhaps narrower in some places. In the dry season, you can wade across as the water is about chest high. In the rainy season, you'd be swept downstream into Lake Nyasa if you were foolish enough to attempt a crossing.

The canoe listed clumsily in the water as an African man, perspiration glistening on his dark face, poled our craft across the river. Evelyn grimaced and shuddered, not at the canoe's perilous journey but at a slithery visitor which observed our progress.

I followed her gaze and noticed the pair of small black eyes of a water snake peering back. I was glad we weren't wading today.

My good friends, Ayubu Mwakalinga, another of the six Kyela District evangelists, and Raymond Atwood, director of missions for the Loudon County

Baptist Association in Tennessee, would certainly agree with that, especially Ayubu.

My mind raced back several months to a scene which still causes Africans in our valley to marvel at God's power.

Ayubu and Raymond were walking through a swampy area in the Kyela District to a remote church. In early 1984 Raymond had come with a team of Baptist preachers and laypersons from America to preach in one of a series of crusades which have made such a tremendous impact on our work in recent years.

Suddenly, a dreaded green mamba dropped from a tree, barely missing Raymond. It landed writhing in front of him. With no thought for his own safety, Ayubu, pushed Raymond to one side, jumped on the snake, and killed it.

But two ugly fangs had gouged into Ayubu's right leg—a frightening prospect for him. A mamba bite is often rapidly fatal, especially in the bush miles away from medical care.

Miraculously, Ayubu recovered after a week of severe pain and countless prayers by Christians in the area. African pagans marveled that God had prevailed over the bite of a snake, a creature so closely associated with the trappings of witchcraft. And they marveled that our *jitihada* (crusade) had recorded 4,119 professions of faith in Jesus, despite the opposition of *Shetani* (Satan).

While they marveled at that, we marveled, even after all these years, at the type of love, so typical of

African Christians, which had caused mild-mannered Ayubu to make such a sacrifice.

That kind of love—and prayer—makes it possible to keep going, despite all the difficulties, tensions, frustrations, and dangers involved in mission work in Third-World countries.

The same kind of love awaited us now on the Malawi side of the Songwe River. Malawians surrounded us, greeting us with respect, enthusiasm, and the three-grip African handshake which vigorously shifts from palm to thumb to palm.

Simoni, whose dedicated work had spread our ministry of evangelism and church planting across the Songwe, introduced us.

"These are our missionaries, Douglas Knapp and his wife," he declared with much fanfare. "They have come to lead our service today." Africans usually call me *Bwana Nepu* (Mr. Knapp) or *Ndugu* (brother) *Nepu*. Evelyn answers to *Mama Nepu* or to *Mama Edsoni* (usually a combination in Swahili of *Mama* and the name of a woman's oldest child).

In this case, our son Edson *(Edsoni)* is the youngest of our four children, but he's the best known in the Kyela District since he grew up there after the older children had gone away to school.

As we continued our trek that day beyond the Songwe, we didn't care what they called us as we happily followed our excited hosts down winding footpaths and through tangled underbrush, anxious to move along with the special event which had led us there.

In a junglelike grove, seventy-five people—speckled by sunlight filtering through oil palms, mango trees, banana trees, and cocoa trees—waited for the special service at a new Baptist church. It had nothing but the shade of the trees to call home.

Five Malawians made professions of faith that afternoon, and crippled seventy-year-old Tomu Mwambalaswa, who had belonged to a Baptist church years ago in Tanzania, hobbled forward joyfully to renew his fellowship.

Then our group trudged to another bend in the Songwe. There thirty-five people formed two lines to be baptized. Simoni and I stood side by side in the chilly water—trusting our slithery friend hadn't followed us—and baptized the new believers simultaneously.

As each ebony face disappeared under the water, I thought how this kind of side-by-side teamwork with Africans has produced remarkable results in evangelism and church planting in the Kyela District. Now it had crossed over the Songwe River into northern Malawi at a point far distant from where Southern Baptist missionaries work in Malawi.

We believe an entire association of churches will develop there as a new growth point to boost the work of Malawi Baptists.

As we told our hosts *kwa heri* (good-bye) and began our trek back to the Tanzanian side of the Songwe, I reflected that the five professions of faith and thirty-five baptisms that day seemed like just a drop in the bucket. But a Swahili proverb proclaims: *"Haba na haba hujaza kibaba"* ("Drop by drop the bucket fills"). It's a simple yet profound concept. Slow, steady drops do fill the bucket.

That's how the Southern Baptist Convention became America's largest evangelical denomination. It grew, drop by drop, from small, rural beginnings in the South in 1845 to fourteen-and-a-half-million members in all fifty states and more than thirty-six hundred foreign missionaries in 106 countries in 1986.

That's how Mary Saunders approached the hunger situation in Ethiopia when she went there in 1985 as a volunteer nurse.

The vastness of the need overwhelmed Mary, even after the twenty-two years she'd served as a missionary to Africa with her husband, Davis, now the Southern Baptist Foreign Mission Board's director for mission work in Eastern and Southern Africa.

Instead of despairing, Mary remembered the Swahili proverb and kept doing what she could, drop by drop, until she began to make a noticeable difference in the lives of starving people. That's how our work has developed in Tanzania over the years as the "drops" have first dripped, then trickled, and then flowed.

The flow became a flood on September 26, 1982, at Ibonde Baptist Church where I baptized 240 people in about four-and-a-half hours. Several churches gathered that day at the Mbaka River about fifteen miles from our home at Makwale (Mah-KWAH-lay) in the Kyela District.

The muddy river bottom sucked at my feet, water spilling down from the Mporoto Mountains chilled my bones, and I baptized until my arms ached. My hands and feet shriveled up from constant exposure to the cold water, but not my spirits.

Africans, in their array of colorful garb, lined the banks, excited and full of the spirit of the occasion, clapping, singing, and punctuating the festivities with the *vigelegele*—a high-pitched, warbling trill women use to show their approval.

Choirs sang vigorously and much too long for my energy. They normally sing a verse between every five baptisms on occasions such as this, but I had them increase that to every ten baptisms so I could survive to baptize again another day.

Periodically, the crowd responded resoundingly when a leader shouted, *"Piga makofi matatu."* They followed his command, "Strike three palms," in vigorous approval of whatever had been said or done. Some think the three sharp claps may have originated as a representation of the Trinity—Father, Son, and Holy Spirit.

Makofi matatus or *vigelegeles* may erupt spontaneously at any time during a sermon, a song, or a baptism in Tanzania. It's a sort of "hallelujah," a way of exclaiming, "You're saying, singing, or doing what we really appreciate."

Joy may seem strange amidst economic deprivation in Tanzania where so many people have so few material things, but it's not strange where God changes lives as He's doing in this East African nation.

That kind of joy reigned that September day at Ibonde Baptist Church as person after person arose, dripping and smiling, and then disappeared into the bush to hand wet baptismal clothing for another person to use.

The day had started on a disquieting note when I had asked one baptismal candidate who his Savior was, and he responded, *"Shetani"* (Satan). Somehow, he'd slipped into the group. We must constantly guard against that in this witchcraft-influenced culture and eliminate the wolves in sheep's clothing. They're not always this easy to spot. We quickly moved him aside for intensive counseling and proceeded with the questioning, hoping the others had a better testimony.

They did. The pastors and evangelists had done their work well. Africans, from *watoto* (children) to *wazee* (respected elder leaders), clearly expressed their salvation experience.

One man's face especially radiated with joy when his pastor asked him if Jesus had changed his life.

"Oh, yes, pastor, now that I have Jesus in my heart, all my friends say I'm a different man. I don't get drunk anymore. I don't beat my wife anymore."

The joy on his wife's face proved the truthfulness of that statement and made a tremendous impact in a culture which treats women as property.

When I first came to Africa as a lay agricultural missionary, I didn't baptize because I'm not a preacher. Even some preacher missionaries won't personally perform baptisms because they think it's culturally better for Africans to do it, rather than give the people the idea it's a special function for white men.

Baptism certainly isn't the special prerogative of

any race or color, and I teach that. But those sorts of distinctions don't seem to bother Africans. I went to a baptismal service during my first term with one of our pastors, Johnstoni Mwaikambo, now an area evangelist.

I thought he would do the baptizing, but he insisted, "No, we want the missionary to baptize."

"I'm sorry, I've never baptized anyone before," I responded. "I'm just a deacon."

"Didn't deacons baptize in the New Testament?" Johnstoni asked.

"Well, I guess they did," I answered and went ahead and baptized twenty-four people.

Since then I haven't worried as much about who should baptize as I have about doing the job in a teamwork effort with African pastors and evangelists. I've been ordained as a deacon, not as a preacher. But I don't feel that's handicapped me. I've never felt the need for further ordination. I suppose I would if I ever felt called as a pastor.

People ask how many I've baptized over the years, but I don't know exactly. It's in the neighborhood of 20,000. I do know that in 1983 I personally baptized more than four thousand of the 5,339 Africans we baptized that year. And I know that between 1978 and mid-1986, Africans and I together immersed at least 33,775 people, many from six simultaneous crusades we'd held just about every two years since 1976.

The crusades, which have used preachers and laypersons from the United States, yielded 26,781 professions of faith in Jesus Christ, including record-shattering totals of 7,505 in 1982 and 12,657 in 1985. We've turned 8,102 of those professions of faith over to other denominational groups, as they requested during counseling.

Meanwhile, Baptist congregations in the Kyela District have increased from forty in 1975 to 250 in 1985, and membership has multiplied sixfold between 1978 and 1985.

All that's a lot when you stop to calculate, but I don't take credit for the converts, baptisms, and churches by myself. I multiply myself through the lives of other people. I do a lot of preaching, personal witnessing, and church development, but I obviously can't get around, win all those people, and start all those churches alone.

My gift is more in planning, leading, and discipling Christians than in evangelism. I select national pastors who have greater gifts than I for preaching and evangelism, and then help train and encourage them to go out and reach people for Christ.

Evelyn and I gained entrée into the lives of Tanzanians through our long tenure of nearly a quarter century in the country and through our agriculture, which has helped improve the quality of life in the area.

Many Africans can't remember the time there hasn't been a "Bwana Nepu." We've lived in Tanzania longer than 50 percent of the native Africans have been alive, due to the short average life span and high birth rate.

That background and recognition factor have allowed us to reach many people. But after a number of years on the mission field, we realized we'd sowed a lot of spiritual seed, but we weren't reaping it effectively in terms of evangelism and church development.

Many Tanzanians are just waiting for someone to come and tell them about the Lord. So that's where we now concentrate our efforts. But we're not coming to them cold. They listen because they know and trust Baptists.

More foreign missionaries, as well as more home missionaries and pastors in the United States, would have better results if they stayed planted in one place longer, built understanding and trust, and let the drops fill the bucket. That's true everywhere but especially where we must cross language and cultural barriers.

But there's another fact to remember when we talk about what it requires to reach people. That's the kind of people God raises up to do the job. God has given us some very gifted African pastors and evangelists who do a tremendous job despite their lack of education and sophistication.

Angesenye Mwakyusa, then pastor of Makwale Baptist Church, did that kind of job a number of years ago in a mud mission church he had the audacity to envision as a lighthouse for God. God honored his audacity, because that's what it turned out to be—a lighthouse.

The young pastor wanted everyone to come to the dedication of the mission of Mawkale church in Ngeleka village. He invited village leaders, govern-

ment officials, Baptist pastors, missionaries, and leaders of other religious groups.

More than five-hundred people flocked there to
dedicate the little mud church. It would hold only
about fifty people, so we gathered out under the
trees.

Angesenye made the occasion a big day for Baptists. We heard one after another of the invited
guests speak, including the leader of the small Muslim community in the area. He stood up and spent
five minutes telling about how Jesus was one of Al-
lah's prophets but that Mohammed was the greatest
prophet.

The crowd sat in silence as Angesenye, the master
of ceremonies, arose. The young preacher didn't lash
out at the Muslim but politely thanked him for his
participation.

Then Angesenye quietly opened his Bible to Mat-
thew 16:15-16 and read the words of Jesus aloud: "He
saith unto them, But whom say ye that I am? And
Simon Peter answered and said, Thou are the Christ,
the Son of the living God."

Angesenye paused and looked up at the congregation—vast for a rural area like ours and full of people
older and more prominent than he.

"Now, who does the Bible say Jesus is?" he asked
softly in Swahili.

A few old men up front responded:

"He is the Christ, the Son of the living God."

Angesenye looked further back into the crowd,
raised his volume, and repeated his question.

A larger group caught on and responded:

"He is the Christ, the Son of the living God."
Angesenye gathered himself for a third thrust.
"Who does God say Jesus is?" he thundered.
The whole crowd roared back:
"He is the Christ, the Son of the living God!"
God's work grows where people know that Jesus
Christ, the Son of the living God, can change lives!

2
Thunder Before the Valley

Night sounds sprang to life from either side of the dusty bush road as we four *wazungu* (whites) trudged into the descending darkness of Tanzania.

Calls of the wild blended in exotic symphony with the thump, twang, and chant of African music and the chatter of *watoto* (children) around outdoor cook fires which crackled and twinkled through the trees.

The bright cook fire on the small *shamba* (farm) of African evangelist Simoni Mwambobe finally melted the ominous darkness and cheered the travelers—especially two persons who'd come from the United States to visit Evelyn and me.

We were weary after a day in the bush and a six-mile *safari* on foot—our disabled, four-wheel-drive vehicle left behind. My fifty-seven-year-old bones ached after the long walk and a lengthy session of baptizing, waist high in the cold current and ankle deep in the muddy bottom of the Songwe River.

We stretched our limbs out in front of Simoni's fire and gratefully accepted the hot *chai* (tea) the Africans thoughtfully had boiled free of parasites in honor of their guests. Even the weariness felt good as

I thought back on the joyful faces of the new converts I'd immersed to symbolize the death, burial, and resurrection of their new Lord and Savior, Jesus Christ.

Then my mind rewound to another time and another body of water more than a half century earlier. If the traumatic experiences of childhood had anything to do with it, I'd never go near the water again to swim or—heaven forbid—baptize people in moving current with uncertain footing and some of God's slithery creatures lurking in the depths.

My earliest recollection of childhood, sometime around my fourth year in the little Florida community of Socrum, about ten miles north of Lakeland, is of Dad holding me up by the feet so icy water could pour out of my lungs. Even then, I couldn't stay away from the water.

We'd gone, in the middle of winter right before Christmas of 1931, to gather firewood near a little creek where Dad liked to fish. He just happened to have his fishing gear along, so naturally he fished. He couldn't stay away from the water, either.

He fished, and I waded, only scarcely hearing his warning not to go out too deep. One moment I was on my feet; the next I floundered, panic stricken, surrounded on all sides by black, icy water.

Dad dropped his fishing pole and made a dive for me. He grabbed me by the hair and pulled. With powerful but loving arms, he lifted me, drained the water from my lungs, wrapped me in his coat, and put me in the safe, warm car.

How wonderful it was to have a father who could

save you from your mistakes—someone in whose
arms you felt safe. My father gave me security when
I needed it. That made it possible later for me to
understand God's relationship as Father to errant
children who need salvation, and it helped implant
the confidence I eventually needed to place myself
in God's care.

That moment came about eight years later, and,
strangely enough, I worried about how my parents
would receive my decision to accept Jesus Christ.
They both had grown up in Christian families, but
neither of them were born-again believers or
churchgoers at that time.

My paternal grandfather, a Presbyterian elder and
New York State judge, was an active churchman and
often preached. All his family, including Dad, felt
like they'd had religion thrust down their throats,
and none of them ended up going to church.

Mom grew up in an Episcopalian family, but she
never went to church now, either. But, somehow,
she became convinced her only child needed to hear
God's Word. She often read the Bible to me, picking
things of interest to a child such as Daniel and the
lion's den, Moses and the burning bush, the New
Testament miracles, and the account of creation.
The idea of God's creation fascinated me, and I used
to think a lot about it.

My mother read me a lot of other books, too, some
rather advanced for my age. People said I had a good
vocabulary as a child because of that.

When I was twelve, a good friend of mine, Charles
Heard, invited me to go to Sunday School with him

at Bethel Baptist Church, a small, country congregation in Socrum. We'd moved back there after living for about four years in Saint Petersburg, where Dad had worked in a landscape nursery after our farm in Socrum had failed because of the Great Depression and disastrous freezes.

We were awfully poor in those days. I remember sometimes having only pants with holes in them to wear and welcomed hand-me-downs from some of Mom's well-to-do relatives. But I guess we were better off than many people, even though Dad had to struggle to get his farm going again.

Holes in the pants embarrassed me terribly but didn't stop me from going to Sunday School the morning Charles invited me. I was excited as we set out on a mile's walk down the country road, dotted with big, beautiful live oaks and orange groves, to the little red-brick church built in the boom times before the Depression struck.

A farmer named Levee Harold taught my Sunday School class. He really knew how to make young boys enjoy studying the Bible. But I guess I didn't really develop a keen interest in spiritual things things until Bethel church called a pastor named C. N. Walker.

Mrs. Walker began teaching me how to play the piano, and I went to the church to practice since we had no piano at home. That gave me plenty of time to talk to Brother Walker, who answered my endless questions with gentle patience.

Gradually, as the weeks passed, my heart began to open up to God like a flower turns to the sun, but I kept resisting. Every Sunday morning as Brother

Walker gave the invitation to accept Christ, I felt a strong urge to respond. I knew I was a sinner and needed God's forgiveness, but it alarmed me when my friends began to go forward to make their professions of faith because that brought it closer to me.

I kept stalling, even though God's urging grew stronger, because I feared my parents would object. With their background in more formal urban churches in the North, they sort of looked down on this little country church.

But they did have plenty of respect for Brother Walker. He came regularly to our home to visit and even got my mother to attend the Woman's Missionary Union meetings. She wouldn't go to worship services, but she enjoyed fellowship with the women.

Finally, on Saturday night, August 7, 1939, I knew I would face the decision again the next morning. As thunder rumbled outside and storm clouds gathered, I began to read the Bible. Then I just lay down on my face on the floor and prayed, asking God to help me. I finally decided to accept Jesus no matter what.

Dad arose each morning about four o'clock, turned on the lights, and came into the kitchen to make coffee. I woke up that Sunday morning and heard him clinking his spoon in his coffee cup.

Normally, I stayed in bed, but not that morning. I got out of bed, went to the head of the stairwell, and stood there indecisively, rubbing the sleep out of my eyes. Then I worked up some courage and hurried downstairs.

There Dad sat, looking surprised but happy to see me. Before I could lose my courage, I blurted out:

"Dad, I want to join the church today."

He looked at me, calmly stirring his coffee, and his eyes locked kindly onto mine. He smiled.

"Well, Doug, I think that would be fine."

He must have wondered why my mouth dropped open. Relief flooded me from head to toe. All those needless fears I'd endured! When Mom woke up and joined us in the kitchen, she responded the same way. I was off to Bethel Baptist Church with a bounce in my step and a joy in my heart not even a gathering storm could dampen.

As I darted down the tree-lined road to church to begin my Christian pilgrimage, thunder rolled overhead on celestial drums—a precursor of the thunder in a distant African valley where that pilgrimage would lead me a quarter of a century later.

Brother Walker baptized me in a small lake near the church three weeks after my profession of faith. My parents came to the baptism and the service. That's the only time I can remember them coming to church, except when I married a beautiful girl named Evelyn Brizzi in 1948 at First Baptist Church in Tampa.

It's hard to believe that wonderful turning point in my life took place only nine years after my baptism. By then much had happened. I'd graduated from Plant High School in Tampa, spent a year and a half in the Navy near the end of World War II, and had finished two years toward an agricultural degree in college.

I was struggling about that time trying to decide whether God wanted me in agriculture or religious work. Several of my friends in the Baptist Student Union at school had surrendered to special Christian service at a student retreat at Ridgecrest Baptist Conference Center in North Carolina. They'd changed their majors to prepare for seminary and church-related careers.

Years later, people began to surrender themselves for a vocational Christian commitment broader than service in a local church, but at that time "special service" carried with it the idea that either you'd preach, direct music or education on a church staff, or at least serve in denominational work. Certainly, Southern Baptists I knew didn't connect agriculture with Christian service.

I prayed about special service because I felt God had a plan for my life and because so many of my friends had responded to calls to special service. *What's wrong with me?* I kept thinking. *Why hasn't the Lord called me?* But I just never felt any clear-cut sense of leading away from agriculture.

One thing, though, left no doubt in my mind—my interest in Evelyn Brizzi.

Carolyn Hirsch, a friend of ours, arranged for us to have a blind date on New Year's Eve of 1947 while we were both home in Tampa for the holidays. Evelyn was a seventeen-year-old freshman at Stetson University in DeLand, Florida, and I was a twenty-year-old junior at the University of Florida in Gainesville.

The blind date began like a vision from above as Evelyn, dazzling in fuchsia lipstick and a fuchsia sweater, came into the living room at her home after I arrived to pick her up.

The evening passed at a New Year's Eve party in a blur of conversation, eating, and adoration. I couldn't take my eyes off her. Just before I took her home, I dared, heart pounding, to bring in the new year with a kiss under the mistletoe. It was wonderful! She kissed me back!

After that, I went to Stetson every weekend to visit her, hitchhiking back and forth about 120 miles round trip from Gainesville to DeLand. I practically camped out there. Some of Evelyn's classmates thought I was a student at Stetson—they saw me around campus so much.

I couldn't stay away, not only because of the electricity we felt when we were together, but also because I became fascinated with her as a unique person.

The more I was with her, the more I thought about her, the more I learned about her, and the more I prayed about her—the more I knew Evelyn was the girl for me.

We had plenty in common. Evelyn's father had lost his electrical firm and then their Tampa home in the financial collapse of the Depression, so both our families knew what it was like to deal with hardship and moving from place to place. In fact, Evelyn had attended twelve different schools in twelve years before entering Stetson, but she still graduated as valedictorian at Plant High School.

Her father had gotten back on his feet as an electrician at MacDill Air Force Base in Tampa, and my father had recouped and owned Knapp's Platt Street Florist Shop and raised his own flowers.

Evelyn's unusual cultural background intrigued me. Her father's family were immigrants from Germany with a mixture of Italian. In fact, her grandmother, Emelia Altendorf Brizzi, in true pioneer fashion, was the only survivor of a shipwreck en route to America.

Grandmother Brizzi and other passengers had floated for days in a small boat. All of them except Emelia had died from exposure and lack of food. She celebrated Shipwreck Day every year until her death because she felt that God had something special for her.

Evelyn's mother was a French war bride from Paris whose father, a Polish immigrant to France, sold clerical supplies to the Roman Catholic Church.

During World War I, Fred Brizzi, Evelyn's father, installed and maintained strategic telephone lines for the Allied forces. But he kept running into difficulty with a French telephone operator who wouldn't give him priority.

Mr. Brizzi got upset because he was stringing vital lines from the front back to high command headquarters, so he set out for Paris to register a complaint. Telephone company officials took him to meet the operator, Suzanne DeLinski, so he could explain the importance of his job.

It was love at first sight for them, just as it was later for Evelyn and me. After that, Mr. Brizzi had no telephone problems and no doubts about whom he would marry.

Evelyn's loving spirit and Christian standards impressed me most. She had accepted Jesus Christ at the age of nine in First Baptist Church of Albuquerque, New Mexico, where her father then worked as a civilian electrical engineer at the Air Force base. They had moved there from Lithia, Florida, Evelyn's childhood home, because her sister suffered from asthma.

Evelyn's father had raised her very strictly and even investigated me before he would let me take her out. Fortunately for me, I passed his scrutiny. An earlier investigation didn't turn out so well, also fortunately for me. Former neighbors in Lithia, where the family lived again after returning from New Mexico, still kid Evelyn about the time Mr. Brizzi flatly refused to let her accept a date with the captain of the high school football team because he didn't approve of the young man.

That suited me fine. I wanted no competition from football team captains—or anyone else.

About two months after we met, we went to the Florida State Fair in Tampa. Suddenly, impulsively, I pulled the car over to the side of the road and began to pour out how I felt about her.

"Darling, more and more I find myself just living for these times when we can be together, dreading leaving you," I blurted out.

"And I spend so much time traveling back and forth to visit you, I don't have time or energy for anything else," I continued, starting to stammer a little. "I've been thinking—Well, couldn't we—I mean it seems like—What I'm trying to say is—Well, shouldn't we think about spending the rest of our lives together?"

Evelyn's eyes captured mine, and I felt my head beginning to spin. Would she think I was a fool?

"Why, Doug! You practically asked me to marry you!"

"Well, I guess I did," I answered, half surprised and totally delighted. "That, er, uh, that just sort of came out. I didn't decide ahead of time to . . ."

She didn't let me finish that sentence. The enthusiasm with which she threw her arms around me and kissed me answered my faltering proposal and sealed my fate. After that, we had an understanding we would marry at the end of the school year.

But we kept it to ourselves a little too long. A few days later, Evelyn bustled around gathering up her belongings to return to Stetson as her ride waited impatiently. Mrs. Brizzi, a worried frown on her face, stopped her daughter on the way out the door.

"Evelyn, you're getting awfully thick with this Douglas Knapp. Don't you think you ought to be more careful of him? You don't even know what his intentions are."

"Of course I know what his intentions are, Mother," Evelyn replied over her shoulder as she rushed out the front door. "He's asked me to marry him, and I've accepted."

Mrs. Brizzi stood there with her mouth open as Evelyn rushed off to school and down a road that eventually would lead to a remote valley in the bush of Tanganyika (then the name for Tanzania) in the shadow of mountains named for pioneer missionary David Livingstone.

3
That Elusive Scent

The road to Tanganyika would take more than fifteen years to travel, and—like the roads in the country itself—had much more than its share of bumper-deep potholes.

Besides facing the tension of choosing between agriculture and a traditional role in ministry, it took me quite awhile to figure out, once I got into agriculture, how it fit into God's will for my life.

He'd led me to do nothing else, it seemed at that point, than to marry Evelyn Brizzi and finish my education. But I guess that was enough to handle for a time. Besides, I knew that a God good enough to give me Evelyn had my best interests at heart. So I tried to wait patiently to see where He would lead.

Meanwhile, Evelyn's parents, satisfied with her father's "investigation" of me, didn't seem worried about us marrying at the end of her freshman year in college, but my parents had reservations, especially Mom.

"Doug, a man just shouldn't marry until he's thirty," she advised repeatedly.

"Mom, I can't wait nine years to marry Evelyn," I pleaded.

"We love each other, and I can still finish school. Just wait 'til you get to know her. You'll love her."

Evelyn helped our cause when she went to work in our florist shop that summer, taking orders, arranging and caring for flowers, and impressing my parents. She quickly added two more Knapp hearts to her collection.

"Doug, how on earth did you find such a pretty, sweet, efficient young lady?" Mom was asking before long. Dad wasn't blind, either, and the victory was ours.

The summer of '48 was wonderful because we could spend every day together. I could hardly wait until she said "I do" on August 27. In the meantime, you might say we kept our romance on ice.

Evelyn often had to go into the large walk-in refrigerator in the back of the shop to get flowers from the large buckets we kept in storage.

"Well, I guess I'd better get some flowers, but those buckets are sure heavy," she'd say with a resigned sound in her voice but a look in her eye meant only for me.

Dad's son wasn't blind, either!

"I'm kind of busy now, Evelyn, but I guess I can take the time to help you move the buckets."

We wondered later if our "polar" excursions really fooled Mom and Dad. Not likely! But one thing is sure. Nothing added more zest to the day than those fleeting kisses amidst the frost and flowers. And noth-

ing made the wait until August 27 seem more endless.

When our wedding day finally came, First Baptist
Church overflowed with many varieties of beautiful
flowers from the walk-in refrigerator where our romance had flirted with frostbite all summer. Dad had
spared no effort for his only son.

But wedding-day jitters almost took their toll. I
went to a side room where grooms prepare to meet
their fate. As I waited happily but nervously for my
cue, Willie, the old church janitor I'd known for
years, slipped into the room.

"Mister Doug, this is your last chance," he whis-
pered furtively. "If you get married, you're going to
have a lot of problems you don't know anything
about now. My advice is to hit the road. Get out of
here while you got a chance."

Willie's advice shook me up for awhile. Then I
regained my composure. The best advice I ever took
was the advice I gave myself at that shaky moment:
ignore every word the well-meaning old man had
said, take my romance off the ice, and get on with
what God was leading me to do. I've never been
sorry.

We honeymooned at a lake in Northern Florida,
stayed for awhile in a small apartment behind the
flower shop, then began our lives together in a small
trailer in Gainesville where Evelyn worked so I could
finish my degree in agriculture.

Everyone should begin married life in a small trailer. It was wonderful. Eleven months after our marriage, we had a new baby, Suzanne, and I had my B.S.

degree from the University of Florida and a scholarship to Ohio State University in Columbus, where I earned a master's degree in horticulture.

After graduation from Ohio State, I made a decision which had mixed results—to work for Dad, making forty-five dollars a week, and live in a cottage at the farm where I had worked as a youth. I raised flowers for the florist business in the daytime and taught adult education in landscaping and gardening several nights a week in the Hillsborough County schools.

The dual experience taught me a lot—but not how to resolve a growing problem with Dad. I loved him very much but had problems working with him.

Dad certainly was not a drunk, but he had an alcohol problem. I've never met a kinder, more generous man than my dad. He'd give things to down-and-out people that his own family needed, and he had higher standards of ethical behavior than many church people I knew.

But he didn't seem to realize how his drinking sapped his drive and befuddled his business judgment. That caused profits from the florist shop and the farm to drop and leave us constantly strapped for money.

"Dad, if you don't straighten this out, I'll have to work somewhere else, so I can have some peace of mind and take care of my family properly," I told him repeatedly.

That hurt because I loved and respected him and had grown up believing children should honor their parents.

"Don't worry, Doug," he'd say. "Things'll be OK."

But they weren't, and he never seriously thought I'd leave. After about three years, I got really discouraged and began to explore other jobs. Finally, I accepted a sales job with Swift and Company in their fertilizer division.

That really shocked Dad, who cut way down on his drinking after that, but I stuck to my decision because it was really best for all of us.

We moved to Winter Haven about forty-five miles east of Tampa, but we kept close ties with my parents. We loved them, despite the problems, and prayed constantly that they would accept Jesus as their Lord and that Dad would stop drinking. I eventually led Mom to Christ before she died from cancer in 1962.

Mom's death overwhelmed Dad with grief because they'd grown very close over the years. We embraced and cried together when I came to the funeral from seminary where Evelyn and I were then preparing for missionary appointment. Dad listened closely for the first time as I told him how Jesus could heal his hurt and change his life. Before I returned to seminary in Kansas City, he agreed to pray about his relationship to God.

Later Dad wrote me in Kansas City and seemed to ask my permission to marry Bernice Bryant, a Christian widow we'd known and respected for years. His gesture touched me deeply, and the prospect of his new life with Bernice brought tremendous relief. Dad would now have someone who loved him to take care of him. Evelyn and I had agonized over his de-

clining health and whether we should go to Africa
and leave him. Missionaries often face the problem
of how to care for ill and aging parents.

Dad and Bernice had a Christian wedding in her
home and began a short but happy life together
before he died in 1967 during our furlough after our
first term of mission service in Africa. He had accepted Christ and completely quit drinking because of
her influence and because of the prayers of many
people after Evelyn and I arrived in Africa in 1964.

But that's running ahead of the story. Eight
months after I left Dad's business, Swift and Company transferred us to Miami. Our family, which had
added Walter in 1951 in Tampa, grew to include
Richard in 1957. But my professional life had its ups
and downs as I struggled to understand what God
wanted me to do.

In 1955, I began a low-paying but fascinating job
as assistant county agent for Dade County—and
eventually got my first whiff of something called
"agricultural missionary." I would follow that faint,
elusive scent for seven more years.

The county called me an "ornamental horticultur-
ist," but the job covered a lot more than that. In fact,
I had all I could handle and then some in working
with farmers, nurserymen, and the general public to
improve farming, gardening, and horticulture.

Always in love with teaching, I hit on the idea of
gardening classes for the public and was swamped
with the response. Some classes had more than five-
hundred students. Then I started classes for specialists such as garden supply dealers, professional gar-

deners (made up mainly of black gardeners in the area), and horticultural spray men. Class relationships led them to develop trade associations in their specialties.

My job really went public when the *Miami News* asked me to write a weekly column, "Plant Doctor," to answer gardening questions, and Channel 10, the local ABC-TV affiliate, asked me to host a five-day-a-week television show, "City Farmer," to take advantage of great local interest in gardening, farming, and horticulture.

Television fascinated me. Some days I'd use film; other days I'd go live in a stand-up talk or interview format with successful gardeners, farmers, nurserymen, dealers, or agricultural specialists.

Live TV had its moments, such as the time I split the seat of my pants working on the set just before air time. I spent the whole thirty-minute show maneuvering my backside away from the camera while cameramen laughed so hard they cried.

"City Farmer" soon became Channel 10's top-rated local morning show, and I spent a lot of time sorting mail and answering phone calls. I thoroughly enjoyed it, except for a few problems.

Sometimes we could literally smell mail coming because people had sent decomposing vegetation and insects for me to analyze. And sometimes, "celebrity" status was a mixed blessing.

One local multiple grafting specialist, a friendly Jewish man I'd used on the show, continually showered me with gifts—mainly overripe fruit he'd sal-

vaged from grocery stores' discards. Sometimes it
was still good. Sometimes it had seen better days.

Once he brought me a bottle of whiskey as a gift.
My refusal left him puzzled and hurt. I didn't want
to offend him and finally pointed out: "You're Jewish.
You should be able to understand. It's against your
religious beliefs to eat pork. I wouldn't expect you to
accept a gift of a ham, because I respect you. It's
against my religious beliefs as a Christian to drink
alcoholic beverages, and I know you wouldn't expect
me to accept a gift of whiskey."

"Ah, my friend, I see," he replied with new ap-
preciation. "You must certainly remain true to your
beliefs."

The crisis passed, and we both remained true to
our beliefs and remained friends. But the crisis continued to build in my spiritual life, even though our
church life couldn't have been better. At one time or
another, I was chairman of the deacons, of the pulpit
committee, and of the steering committee; I sang in
the choir and led Sunday School and Training Union
(now Church Training) Departments.

But we still felt something was missing. Then, at
long last, a glimmer of light appeared. The year I
joined the county agent's office, the Southern Baptist
Convention's annual meeting convened in Miami.
That's where our first scent of agricultural missions
briefly, tantalizingly surfaced.

A missionary doctor from Nigeria, speaking on
Missions Night at the Convention, told how he
reached people for Christ after he helped relieve
their suffering.

Sitting far out in the auditorium, engulfed by the huge audience, I had a sensation God had zeroed in on me and was saying: "I can use you as a farmer on the foreign mission field. You can teach hungry people to feed themselves and then teach them how to come to Me."

I didn't hear anything the rest of the evening. God took over, and His message became more and more intense. I'd never heard of a missionary farmer, but I had to find out about it.

After the service, I took Evelyn by the hand and hurried to the front of the auditorium to ask someone about it.

To our surprise, we found Millard Berquist, our former pastor in Tampa, seated on the platform. He'd always declared I should be a preacher. But God had never told me that, and I had continued to search. Now Dr. Berquist had entered the scene again and probably wondered why I still couldn't understand God's will.

"Is there any such thing as a farmer missionary?" I blurted out after a quick hello.

"Well, I don't know, Doug, but we'll find out," he responded.

He introduced us that night to Elmer West, then the director of the Missionary Personnel Selection Department at the Southern Baptist Foreign Mission Board in Richmond, Virginia.

I came right down to business with Dr. West.

"Could the Foreign Mission Board use me as a missionary farmer?"

Dr. West fielded the question smoothly, gracefully, and noncommittally.

"Well, our Board doesn't have any openings like that now," he answered. "But we recognize there's a great need in this area. Maybe, we'll have an opening in the future."

He gave us a form.

"Fill this out, with all the facts about your experiences, your church relationships, and your testimony, and we'll keep it on file. If anything comes up, we'll get in touch with you."

Of course it would come up! God, Who has advance word over the Foreign Mission Board on these matters, had just told me He wanted me as an agricultural missionary. But the Lord and the Foreign Mission Board move in strange and mysterious ways. The days grew into weeks. Then months passed; then years!

Eventually, in 1959, I passed what I thought was the age limit for career appointment. The scent of the missions trail rapidly downgraded from elusive to nonexistent.

Life went on, but I still couldn't understand God's call because I thought He'd spoken so clearly that night at the Southern Baptist Convention meeting four years earlier.

Meanwhile, our three children continued to grow, and my mind's eye can still replay scenes of them through those years.

They're vivid scenes of Richard, now a pathologist, shaking his beautiful golden ringlets as he snuggled in his mother's arms; Walter, now a concert-level pianist, struggling at age five to learn his home address and then picking it up at once when Evelyn turned it into a song; and Suzanne, our feminine but energetic nine-year-old, determinedly pushing a power mower across our carefully landscaped, quarter-acre corner lot.

Suzanne, now a missionary to Ethiopia, became quite an expert in horticulture in those days. I've always enjoyed taking long baths for relaxation. Sometimes dinner guests arrived before I was through, and Suzanne would show them the garden and all the rare plants we had there. She'd listened to me give the tour so often she could do it by heart, calling each flower by name and telling something about it. It really impressed people that this little girl knew so much.

Suzanne practically grew up with us. She was born when Evelyn was nineteen. In later years, people often mistook them for sisters.

Recently, Suzanne reminisced about her childhood and recalled things I didn't realize impressed her so much.

"Daddy has always loved children and loved to play games with us," she said. "He's still very much of a child at heart himself. He always bought us Christmas presents with himself in mind, and he always knew how to make children happy.

"In our neighborhood, Daddy was sort of a 'Pied Piper' with the kids. Every weekday afternoon, he had what he called 'Uncle Doug's Playtime.' All the kids in the neighborhood came, and Daddy made up games for us, like 'Alligator.' He'd be the alligator and chase us between two bases.

"Then, on Saturdays, the kids came and worked with 'Uncle Doug' in his magnificent yard full of tropical plants he'd brought back from overseas gardening tours.

"As a reward, he'd spin elaborate stories which fascinated us, putting each child in a specific role, no matter how many children were there. We loved that and begged for more. Sometimes he'd tell continuing stories, building the suspense until the next time.

"Daddy also shared exciting ideas. I grew up preferring adult conversation and would often listen to my father talk instead of going out to play. I preferred male conversation. Women had nothing on Daddy in their talk of recipes and babies. I'd rather hear him talk of exotic plants or global concerns."

It's surprising what a child remembers about parents. Evelyn and I still look back fondly on those growing years as good years with our children. But, even so, we still remember it as a time we could neither understand nor escape God's call.

Eventually, I left the county agent's office and went to work for a major chemical firm as their field representative at twice the salary and more than twice the problems. For the first time, we had enough money to live comfortably, but it didn't make me happy. I didn't like a number of aspects about the job, including having to take customers to night clubs and set up hospitality rooms where they could drink.

The spiritual ferment redoubled.

Maybe God wanted us in some other kind of full-time Christian work now that foreign missions seemed out of the question.

Maybe I should preach, as Dr. Berquist had long suggested, but how could I manage to train for a new career now? It was expensive to raise three children, buy a house, and pay off debts.

Our prayers brought no clearcut answers, likely because of my mental reservations.

I'd pray: "Lord, show me Your will."

But, in the back of my mind, I'd almost subconsciously add: "If I like it, maybe I'll do it."

God wants our whole commitment, not fragments of it.

We struggled through this phase for about two years. Then, in the summer of 1962, John Wheeler, our pastor, and his wife, Kay, our music director, asked us to go with them to Ridgecrest Baptist Conference Center. They had prayed with us and thought the trip might help us sort things out. We later learned they also were dealing with a call to foreign missions.

Ridgecrest must be one of God's favorite places to get down to business. That's where He got through to my friends from Baptist Student Union days at the University of Florida, and that's where He finally penetrated my thick skull.

He used a banker-turned-music-director to do it.

Suddenly, the man who then directed music for the Missouri Baptist Convention stopped in the middle of a class he was teaching on song leading and seemed to look right at me.

"I think you need to hear my testimony," he interjected, sweeping his hand over the group. He didn't point his finger at me literally but did so figuratively.

"Several years ago, I began to feel God leading me away from banking into a full-time Christian music ministry," he said. "I had a family and didn't see how I could afford to go back and get the training I would need. So I put it off. Then, one day, I suddenly lost my job and didn't know what to do."

He paused. Then he continued.

"That shook me up, but then I began to realize God had pushed me out of my security so I could do what He wanted me to do. I went to seminary, and God opened the way for me. I've been happy ever since."

Then the music director delivered a verbal blow, like a jab to the solar plexus, that really hit me.

"Don't fail to obey God! You'll always regret it if you do. And remember, if anybody here hesitates to give themselves to the Lord's will because of financial concerns, be assured that where God leads, He provides."

The preacher, the following Sunday morning, delivered the follow-up blow, a right cross to the heart, when he powerfully and poignantly preached on the rewards of giving your life to special service.

Here I was again, dealing with "special service" as I had in college. God wanted me to have the faith to turn loose and leave the rest up to Him, even if I didn't know how to use agriculture in Christian work.

Then the preacher threw me a curve. He extended the closing invitation for special service only to young people, just as I was about to go forward.

That stopped me in my tracks but not in my decision. Evelyn and I turned around and knelt in the pew and prayed.

I said, "Lord, if You'll show us what You want us to do, we'll do it." No reservations this time.

A sense of God's presence overwhelmed us as we arose to leave and began to look around for Suzanne. My eyes swept the crowd, and I finally spotted our daughter up front among the young people who had responded to the invitation.

God had struck again. Suzanne had surrendered to missions in the same service where I finally turned loose of my stubborn will.

Still floating in the euphoria of our decision, we returned to Miami, ready to quit my job and follow where God would lead.

I kicked off my shoes, dropped onto the couch and began shuffling through the mail which had accumulated during our trip.

Suddenly, I let out a whoop, and Evelyn looked up, startled. We love to get mail, but usually it's no shouting matter.

"Doug, what on earth's the matter with you?" she exclaimed.

"This!" I waved a letter at her.

The postmark said, "Richmond, Va.," and the signature said, "Elmer West," but I thought surely the

Lord Himself had written it on Foreign Mission Board stationery and mailed it directly from heaven.

"We have your name on file," the letter said, "as one who has expressed an interest in missions in the field of agriculture, and we have requests from missionaries in three different areas of the world who want someone with your background and training . . ."

The letter dropped out of my hand, unfinished. I was so excited I was ready to report the next day.

But my good friend and counselor, Millard Berquist, brought me back to reality. Dr. Berquist had moved to the presidency of Midwestern Baptist Theological Seminary in Kansas City, Missouri, from his pastorate in Tampa since we talked to him on the platform of the Southern Baptist Convention in 1955.

The unfinished letter at my feet, I had him on the telephone telling him Evelyn and I would soon arrive there for study.

Dr. Berquist didn't sound surprised to hear what God had done. He interpreted it as my finally giving in to the call to preach. But, as a former Foreign Mission Board trustee, he knew it wouldn't be that easy.

"Now, slow down, Doug. We want you and Evelyn to come to Midwestern, but don't you think you'd better contact the Foreign Mission Board first and find out if you qualify for appointment?"

"What do you mean 'qualify'? Doesn't the letter say . . . ?"

Then I finished reading it. Dr. West wasn't hiring

me on the spot but simply asking if I felt God's call to make application for appointment. Candidates for appointment, we would later learn, travel an intensive road from application to appointment.

The Board had raised the age limit to thirty-five for career appointment (and has raised it again since). That's how old I was, even before entering the appointment process or going to seminary to complete the thirty semester hours of study then required of lay specialists.

And then Bill Dyal, one of the Board's personnel consultants, laid another reality on us.

"Doug, you have a teenage daughter, and we don't appoint families with teenagers because many teenagers have problems adjusting to life overseas," he said as gently as possible.

But he added: "Let's go through the system, the investigation, and see what happens."

"*Sometimes,*" he said, stressing that word, "the personnel committee makes an exception if it seems proper in an individual case. But don't take it for granted. It doesn't often happen."

That threw more than a little doubt on appointment as a Southern Baptist missionary, but no doubt on our resolve to serve God in agriculture.

I resigned my job and enrolled in doctoral study in agriculture at the University of Florida. If the Foreign Mission Board decided against us, then I would qualify to teach in a Christian university.

Some would say I was a little hasty in resigning so quickly. It's not usually a wise move so early in the appointment process. But I had decided to follow

God with no mental reservations. I'm fortunate the situation worked out as it did.

Just as the music director at Ridgecrest had said, God began to take care of our needs—in more ways than one.

Despite a depressed market caused in Florida by the Cuban missile crisis, we sold our house—almost immediately. A Christian woman offered to store our furniture, and a local businessman gave us a little money.

The most important way God cared for us involved the Board's appointment process. It revealed that our qualifications perfectly fit an urgent need in East Africa, and Suzanne could go directly to a stable situation in a school in Kenya which based its curriculum on the American system.

God's strange and mysterious ways had harmonized with the Board's. The personnel committee, after careful deliberation, decided to appoint us even though Suzanne and I would be a little over the normal age when we arrived in East Africa. They ruled in favor of Suzanne because of her maturity and the school situation there.

Evelyn and I wouldn't have been bitter if the Board had turned us down because we're glad it cares about the welfare of children. But we're also glad it will make an occasional exception.

That exception sent us packing off to Midwestern Seminary after the semester ended at the University of Florida.

Kansas City's hard winter hit us warm-blooded Floridians like a sledgehammer. We arrived in the midst of bitter cold, but with the joy of springtime in our hearts and a promise of a seminary study loan from the Foreign Mission Board in our pockets.

Our kids looked as startled as African children who see white people for the first time. Snow—that cold white stuff—coated their new world. They'd only read about it or heard about it in the tall tales told in "Uncle Doug's Playtime."

It fascinated them. They pelted each other with cold, hard snowballs while Evelyn and I examined the cold, hard realities we faced.

The euphoria of Ridgecrest had begun to fade.

Evelyn needed thirty semester hours of credits, too, because she'd completed only one year at Stetson University before our marriage. She needed at least two years or sixty semester hours to qualify for appointment as a missionary wife.

So she struggled to get back in the swing of studying while holding her own as one of only two women enrolled in classes that year.

But time would prove she hadn't been valedictorian of her high school graduating class for nothing. She excelled at Midwestern, just like she's excelled at anything she's tried. (Later, after years on the mission field, she worked out a study program with the University of South Florida in Tampa and graduated with distinction in 1985 with a B.S. degree in African studies.)

We faced intense academic pressure at Midwestern combined with the stresses of caring for three children, juggling slim finances, and living in a rather grim neighborhood.

It was one of those times along the trail to foreign missions when we had to fall back on our deep, personal conviction that God had called us there for a reason. No one should ever embark on such a pilgrimage without that assurance. The time ahead would test our faith, endurance, personal relationships, sense of call, and sense of humor.

Housing became the first test. There was none.

Lavell Seats, then Midwestern's professor of missions and dean of students, took pity on us and found us temporary quarters in a farmhouse. He brought us pots, pans, dishes, and other items from his own house to use until we became settled.

Then he asked, "Would you be willing to live in a low-rent housing project? It's the only thing we can find."

What does a struggling seminary student do but take the only available option? Thus, Dr. Seats and the Lord—not necessarily in that order—introduced us to our first real mission field: Kansas City's version of skid row.

Evelyn's heart sank, and I gulped at the sight of the dingy, run-down neighborhood which seemed light-years away from our beautifully landscaped home in suburban Miami.

The onetime respectable Italian neighborhood, now deep in the throes of urban rot, housed a mixture of low-income blacks, down-and-out whites, and a variety of other ethnic groups.

We sidestepped wine-soaked human derelicts and warily watched swaggering young punks as we made our way to our new home as inconspicuously as possible. But Suzanne, a blossoming thirteen-year-old, attracted attention despite herself in that neighborhood. Mr. Brizzi's strong protectiveness of Evelyn didn't even approach my fierce determination to shield Suzanne.

The inner city seemed like a desert to a family which enjoyed classical music, ornamental horticulture, fine arts, and conversation with educated people. But then so would Makwale, Tanzania, where God has taught us that there's more to the quality of life than plush surroundings or intellectual stimulation.

He began that lesson in Kansas City, a period in our life in which we learned much more than theology and Bible. God pierced our hearts the first time we looked into the eyes of one of those derelicts and saw a human being desperately in need of love, a human being as important to God as any of our friends.

God taught us what it really means to give a cup of cold water in His name when we brought food to poor, elderly people whose lives depended on it.

He taught us that those who follow Him must be doers of His word and not just hearers and proclaimers of it. That understanding became a cornerstone of our ministry in Tanzania where we combine physical and spiritual assistance to people who suffer a severe shortage of both.

God also taught us a deeper level of the joy that comes when someone accepts Jesus Christ as Lord and Savior. We had won people to Christ in our churches back in Florida. Now we crossed racial and cultural barriers to do it. That made serving Him special.

We had prided ourselves that we weren't racists like many whites we knew, even though my maternal grandfather had been a Confederate colonel, and my grandmother had once owned seventy-five slaves.

But God put that to the test in Kansas City before we went to Africa and prepared us really to understand that He's no respecter of persons, and that He looks on the heart and not the outward appearance.

We fell in love with the little black children who came to our apartment to play with unreserved enthusiasm after they got to know us.

"Uncle Doug's Playtime" went into reruns for a new audience. It fascinated them even more than it had the middle-class white children back in the suburbs of Miami, who had so much more in their lives than these deprived inner-city children in Kansas City.

We used it as a path into their lives and the lives of their families to bring them the message that Jesus Christ loves them. Gradually, the message took root and lives began to change.

Twelve-year-old Danny, who had a mother who walked the streets and no father, made that change in our living room one dark, stormy afternoon near the end of our stay in Kansas City.

He knelt to make his profession of faith as the storm reached the peak of its fury, oblivious to everything but the joy of his newfound faith.

As thunder reverberated between the low-rent houses, I choked back the tears and thought of another twelve-year-old boy who had raced down a tree-lined road in Socrum, Florida, on a thundery day back in 1939 to turn his life over to Jesus Christ.

God has a plan for Danny's life just like He did for me back then—and still does, I thought. Then I prayed that He would lead us both where He wanted us to go.

As the little black children came into our lives, we naturally wanted to take them to our church. Since our church had no black members, we asked the pastor about it, and he told us to bring them anytime.

So, on the opening day of Vacation Bible School, we joyfully led a large, multicolored procession of children to church.

The church, like the neighborhood, had once prospered. Now, as the neighborhood changed, the congregation struggled to survive. We discovered too late that the old guard in its midst was fighting a rear guard action against becoming "tainted" by the community.

The young pastor, extremely embarrassed, came to me and asked me not to bring the children back to Bible School. An important deacon of the church had said he would resign his membership if "those people come to *my* church again."

"If I have to be in heaven with people like that," he added, "I'd rather be in the other place."

Those were dangerous words for a deacon to utter in the presence of a God whose Holy Word says,

If anyone says, "I love God," yet hates his brother, he is a liar. For anyone who does not love his brother, whom he has seen, cannot love God, whom he has not seen. And he has given us this command: Whoever loves God must also love his brother (1 John 4:20-21, NIV)!

Nevertheless, the young pastor apologetically said, "We really can't afford to lose this man from our church. We're barely making it as it is. Please don't bring those children back."

Stifling a response that the church certainly could afford to lose that man, I agreed. I did so for the sake of the children and the fellowship of the church, but especially for those precious children who thought all Christians loved them.

We went to another church where the children experienced the joy of a brand-new, enriching experience. No one said a negative word to crush their spirits.

As a Southerner who had lived with racism, I'd never expected to experience it in a midwestern church. But God taught me that racism is a condition of the human heart which knows no boundaries.

We've found it entrenched even between different black tribes in Africa—sometimes to the point of bloody confrontation. That kind of tribalism contributes to many of the problems faced by African nations.

And we've experienced racism in reverse in Africa. One Christmas Eve, while Evelyn lay in a hospital in Nairobi, Kenya, our son, Edson, then ten years old, and I got a taste of what prejudice against a minority is like.

We stayed at the hospital as long as possible and then headed back to our room in a Methodist guest house, the only place we could find after an emergency flight from Tanzania that morning.

The buses had stopped running, and we didn't have a car, so we caught a ride in a *matatu*, an African version of a taxicab.

You'd have to see a *matatu* to believe it. It's a covered pick-up-truck-type vehicle run by Africans for Africans. They jam the passengers in like sardines and then zip in and out of Nairobi traffic like a whirling dervish with passengers hanging out the back door.

The passengers that night probably never had seen whites in a *matatu*, and some didn't like the idea much.

"Who do those rich *wazungu* think they are riding in our *matatu?*" a drunk man spat out in Swahili, not realizing we could understand. "We ought to kill them right now for coming to our country and taking all the good jobs. I killed *wazungu* during the Mau Mau rebellion."

Edson and I sat silently, our hearts pounding. We consoled ourselves with the fact the *matatu* was so jam-packed with people that no one could move, much less mount an attack.

Then an African woman spoke up.

"Don't you talk like that. They haven't taken our jobs. Have you forgotten that white people have done a lot of things to help us? And you don't know anything about them. They're probably very fine people. You leave them alone."

Things quieted down, and Edson and I got off at our stop, thankful that a black woman in this male-dominated culture had the courage to speak. I reflected sadly on how some American whites had failed to oppose Ku Klux Klan atrocities against blacks.

About two years earlier, Edson, who grew up playing with African children, had another difficult experience on the mission field. One day he came running into our house looking for Evelyn and sobbing:

"Mother, my friends don't want to play with me. They say I've got hair like a cat and skin like a pig."

I guess that's the way Africans see us, at least until they get used to us. A cat's hair is short and straight. A white pig's hair is sparse and the pinkish skin underneath resembles that of a white person.

Edson and the African children, who became embarrassed over the way they'd treated their friend, worked out the problem. He and African children got along well over the years and loved each other.

One of the African boys who taunted Edson, a young man named Safe (SAH-fay), is still his best friend. They correspond with each other and enjoy each other's company whenever Edson visits.

Apparently neither experience damaged Edson, who dreams of returning to Tanzania as a missionary after finishing college and seminary.

But it taught us all how to empathize with the pain racism of any kind brings to people who suffer it. It deadens proclamation of Christian love wherever it flourishes.

4
One Bite at a Time

"Tanganyika Revolts."

That's what the banner headline said—and we were on the way right into the middle of it!

We'd just settled down in our seats on a Swissair flight ferrying us to Zurich on the first leg of our trip to East Africa in early January, 1964.

A pretty young flight attendant offered us a newspaper with a cheerful smile but drew back, flustered at my startled expression.

I had reason to be startled. The Tanganyikan armed forces had launched a revolt against their commanding officers and President Julius Nyerere. If the doors of the plane hadn't already closed, we might have gotten right off. Our call to missions was getting frightening.

An enjoyable family Christmas in 1963 had soothed the tensions of a year full of challenge, and we'd wondered what could be more difficult. We'd soon find out.

The day after Christmas, Bill Lewis, pioneer missionary to the Nyakyusa people in Tukuyu, Tanganyika, had visited Tampa during his furlough and filled us with visions of the great things we could do if we'd come work in Rungwe District with him and his wife, Nina.

We got so excited we wrote to the field and said we didn't have to wait until we got to Africa to decide where we'd work. We would work with the Lewises.

But the Baptist Mission of East Africa, which then covered work in three countries, wisely slowed us down. Mission chairman James Hampton wrote to say other missionaries in Tanganyika, Kenya, and Uganda would want to tell us about other opportunities. James, who became associate director for East Africa in later years, urged us to wait, survey the situation after we arrived, and pray about it before deciding.

We agreed and eagerly anticipated the survey trip James said we could take through East Africa after Swahili language study in Dar es Salaam, Tanganyika.

That anticipation suddenly receded sharply. Tanganyika was in revolt—and we weren't even there yet!

During our year in Midwestern Seminary, our systems had already had more excitement than we could stand, including the time we narrowly missed a shoot-out in our neighborhood, which had left bullet holes and blood stains on our front porch.

A raging blizzard had stranded us in the mountains with a desperately sick child enroute to Florida from Kansas City after finishing seminary. And we'd escaped disaster in Canada when we barely avoided the clutches of bears.

The bear episode came during a family vacation between semesters at seminary on a trip to show thirteen-year-old Suzanne, eleven-year-old Walter and six-year-old Richard something of North America before they arrived on a new continent.

Our family looks back on that trip as a wonderful time together, despite the bears. We camped out and cooked on a wood stove in Jasper National Park. We loved Canada, and Evelyn enjoyed cutting her own wood and cooking on that stove—not realizing a wood cookstove lay in her future on our remote station in Tanganyika.

But she didn't enjoy the encounter with the bears and still has a back injury which reminds her of it.

Bears up there are notorious for raiding food supplies and, quite inhospitably, show no more regard for tourists than they do for their fellow Canadians.

As we relaxed near our tent, a warning went out that bears were coming. That jolted our serenity and sent us scurrying from our campsite.

We should have just run and let the bears have our food, but struggling seminary students don't give up their next meal easily. So Evelyn and Walter each grabbed a handle of our food chest, took one frightened look over their shoulders, and "lit out" like a pack of bears was after them.

As they ran, Evelyn's right arm got tired, and she puffed to a stop.

"Let's change sides, Walter," she urged, anxious to resume the flight.

She jerked the chest up quickly with her left arm and crumpled in agony, as back muscles violently pulled loose. We lifted her and put distance between us and the bears, who finally got distracted and ignored us.

Evelyn spent a week in a hospital and has had recurring back problems ever since. She has to exercise regularly and never travels anywhere without muscle relaxers and painkillers to use in an emergency.

About ten years later in Africa, we would make a similar desperate flight from a herd of elephants rumbling through the remote bush country in the dark toward our jacked-up car.

The car had ground to a halt for a seventeenth time—and that's the truth—with a flat tire. As we struggled to get the tire off the rim and patch it again, we heard loud crashing noises in the distance like trees being knocked down, and then the trumpeting of elephants.

Then we saw the hulks lumbering through the dark—directly at us.

We made a mad dash into the car, forgetting it was on a jack. But fifteen-year-old Richard, who turned out to be the hero, didn't forget.

Operating with the same efficiency he now shows as a physician, he frantically lowered the jack, threw it inside and jumped in after it—upset that his family had left him to do that dangerous chore alone.

We got out of there on three tires, a rim, and prayer, barely escaping the elephants. We drove that way the rest of the night.

It's a good thing we didn't know about the elephants and countless other adventures and misad-

ventures which lay ahead as we read of revolt in
Tanganyika. God reveals the tribulations of following
Him in bite-sized chunks. But sometimes they seem
like more than a mouthful.

Eight hours after news of revolt greeted us on the
runway of Idlewild Airport in New York City, we
landed in Switzerland: bewildered, lonely, and
frightened.

The beautiful sight of our dear friends John and
Kay Wheeler, who had preceded us to the field as
missionaries, had the same effect on us as pouring
water on a dry sponge.

We stayed with them in Ruschlikon, where John
taught at the Baptist seminary, and had a chance to
relive our pilgrimage together—from John's days as
our pastor to the trip to Ridgecrest in 1962, to missionary appointment, and to this moment of uncer-
tainty about the future.

Several days later, we began the pilgrimage again
with renewed conviction that God had brought us
this far, and no African revolt would stop us. By the
time we arrived in East Africa, President Nyerere
had regained control of Tanganyika, and the situation had stabilized.

As the years have presented one crisis after another, we've learned that missionaries sometimes do
face dangers, but headlines in America often make
the scene seem more grim and widespread than it
actually is.

Headlines about America in Africa create the same
effect. Africans who read about America's civil rights
battles of the 1960s urged missionaries not to return

there for furlough. They thought the whole country
was in flames.

Even so, difficulties, crises, and hardships have
been constant companions. Between the two us,
Evelyn and I have had hepatitus, typhoid fever, malaria, an amoebic abscess of the liver, relapsing fever,
and a bleeding ulcer.

We've spent the night in mosquito-infested
swamps, been capsized in a canoe, held at spear
point by drunk tribesmen, marooned by floods,
trapped for thirteen weeks by a cholera quarantine,
and stuck up to our Land Rover's headlights many
times during rainy season in rivers of mud called
roads.

I suffered only flash burns—with no scars—when a
kerosene refrigerator blew up in my face. And Evelyn has thwarted an attack by armed robbers, rein-
jured her back pulling a flaming gas stove out of the
wall, and almost died from the amoebic abscess.

Our first grandchild, Joylene Groce, did die of
complications from diarrhea in Ethiopia where our
daughter and her husband are missionaries. That
happened in March 1972, about three months after
Evelyn's father died. (Her mother died the following
year.)

The deaths broke our hearts, but they brought us
closer to the Africans who live in stark conditions and
confront death constantly.

Even though accustomed to death, Africans feel
the same grief we feel. They brought us gift after gift
of eggs, coffee, and even money. From their poverty,

they wanted to express their sympathy for us, even though they regard all whites as rich.

The spiritual highlight came the day after Evelyn's father died when twenty-one pastors and church leaders came to visit and hold a memorial service in our living room with hymns, prayers, Scripture, and a sermon. Afterwards, they took up a love offering for us. It was less than two dollars, but it was the largest offering we'd seen given up to that point by these people in a single service.

We couldn't refuse a gift of love, even though we felt unworthy to receive it, knowing it came from such needy people. Similarly, Christians can't refuse God's call to missions because of danger.

Joylene's death was extremely painful to us, but we realize dangers, tragedies, and illnesses can strike people anywhere, even in modern, developed America. When we experience the difficulties of life while following God's calling, we know they're never in vain and that missionaries aren't exempt.

Missionaries have faced difficulties throughout the history of Southern Baptist foreign missions, and some haven't survived, beginning with Dr. J. Sexton James, our first medical missionary. He and his wife, Annie, died when their ship sank in a typhoon off the coast of China in April, 1848.

Illness, especially in the early days of missions, also has taken its toll over the years.

One of the appeals that tugged at the heart of Dr. T. W. Ayers before he went as a Southern Baptist medical missionary to China in 1900 was the tragic death of three children in one missionary family during an epidemic, possibly of cholera. Cholera, malaria, smallpox, yellow fever, and other diseases killed many early missionaries and their families. Africa was once known as "the white man's grave."

In fact, in the history of medical missions, early missionary doctors weren't thought of as missionaries in the true sense of the word, but rather as persons sent to the mission field to take care of the "real" missionary and his family. That changed as mission boards learned the value of medical missions in its own right, just as they later learned the value of agriculturists and other missions specialists.

Mission-field-related illnesses can still strike, such as with the death of Dudley Phifer of Malawi and Transkei in 1980 and Larry Thomas of Tanzania in 1982. And missionaries face the possibility of violent death.

We sadly recall such mission field tragedies as the deaths of Rufas F. Gray in a Japanese prisoner-of-war camp in the Philippines in 1942, Bill Wallace in a Communist prison in China in 1951, Wimpy Harper in a drowning accident in Tanzania in 1958, Eric Clark while hunting cape buffalo in Kenya in 1968, Mavis Pate in an Arab guerrilla ambush in Gaza in 1972, Archie Dunaway at the hands of Communist-backed guerrillas in Zimbabwe in 1978, and James Philpot, gunned down in 1985 in Mexico City after an automobile accident.

That looks frightening collected in one place. But it looks different when we take it from the perspective of more than 140 years of Southern Baptist foreign missions history.

Miraculously, we know of only thirty-eight of our foreign missionaries out of 8,808 appointed through the end of 1985 who have died violently. Causes of eighteen other deaths, mostly from early missions years, are unknown.

Only ten missionaries in all those years are known to have died by violence other than accident, from the murder of J. Landrum Holmes in 1861 in China to James Philpot's death 124 years later. Holmes died while attempting to persuade invaders not to attack a village.

Thousands of missionaries over those years have lived and worked in the world's danger spots and survived with God's protection. The safest place on earth is where God wants you.

That sounds like a missionary cliché, but it isn't. Again and again over our career, we've realized the truth of the assertion that "all things work together for good to them that love God, to them who are called according to his purpose" (Rom. 8:28).

But, in the beginning, as we left John and Kay Wheeler in Switzerland and headed toward the unknown, we hadn't even begun to explore the depths of that concept.

Blissfully ignorant of all the different kinds of dangers but assured we were going where God wanted us, we landed in Nairobi, Kenya—our first stop in Africa before traveling on to Dar es Salaam.

The Nairobi scene assaulted our senses with its unique blend of African, Asian, British, Third World, First World, urban, and rural characteristics.

Along with a variety of European and American

tourists, we gawked at beautiful Asian women, swathed in saris, and at bearded, turbaned Sikhs. We marveled at leathery, sunbaked British expatriate residents left over from colonial days, and we admired Africans in colorful traditional dress, safari clothing, snappy business suits, or ragged hand-me-downs.

The multicolored, many-cultured throng flowed in an endless, shoulder jostling, aromatic bustle down the streets of this city of contrasts.

Within minutes we could walk from a scene of modern refinement at the New Stanley Hotel, where Ernest Hemingway once socialized at the hotel's famed Thorntree sidewalk restaurant with his colleagues, to quaint, narrow Bazaar Street. There we found numerous small Indian shops and a profusion of colorful merchandise and pungent odors of coffee, spices, and perfumes of the East. They say you can buy anything you want on Bazaar Street, now called Biashara Street, and we believe it.

About a mile further, we could explore a seemingly rural African area where people from small bush towns and villages maintained their old ways.

Then, fifteen minutes' drive to the edge of town would bring us to the heart-rending Mathari Valley slum area where one-hundred-twenty-five thousand persons, in families made up of a dozen or so members each, crowd into makeshift nine-by-twelve-foot cardboard hovels with dirt floors and no electricity or sanitary facilities.

Thousands of Africans flood even now into the city

to squat and await the riches of urban life which seldom come.

While we coped with that kind of culture shock in our new world, we faced an even more severe jolt. We would have to travel on to Dar es Salaam and leave Suzanne behind at Rift Valley Academy (RVA) in Kijabe, about thirty miles out of Nairobi. We'd agreed with Cornell Goerner, then the Foreign Mission Board's secretary for Africa, that Suzanne would board at RVA, a school for MKs (missionary kids) run by the African Inland Mission. Parting wasn't easy for us or her—especially her.

Many MKs have had a great experience at Rift Valley Academy, but Suzanne never liked boarding school. She begged to stay every time she came to Tanganyika for three, month-long holidays between terms. But, as far as we knew then, there weren't other alternatives for a child her age.

We learned later that Suzanne, because of her own sensitive spirit and call to missions, tried extra hard to make it at the academy despite her unhappiness, because she felt that if she didn't make it, we wouldn't make it as missionaries. Looking back, we realize that was quite a burden for a teenager to carry. Thankfully, compensations lay in store for her.

Each time we parted or read one of her letters, tears came to our eyes. But then things improved somewhat. Walter was soon old enough to enroll in Rift Valley Academy. His arrival there, after a year at the International School of Dar es Salaam while we studied Swahili, made it easier for both Suzanne and Walter. They became strong allies at school.

But the arrival of V. Lynn Groce in Africa revolutionized Suzanne's whole attitude.

Lynn, a lean, good-looking young man with a sharp intellect, a quick smile and dark, penetrating eyes, came out as an agriculturist to work with Evelyn and me under the Foreign Mission Board's two-year Journeyman program.

He quickly showed he had ability, spiritual depth, and a heart for missionary work when he started one of the first churches which grew out of our ministry.

It all started after he led a one-legged *mzee* (respected elder leader) to Christ amidst the swirling dust beside the rutted, winding bush road to Ikulu village.

As the old man prayed to receive Christ, a couple of other African men stood by listening and shuffling their bare feet in the dust, impressed in typical African manner that an old man was making such a decision. Most Africans revere gray hair which signals wisdom, leadership, and a storehouse of indispensable knowledge.

"We'd like to do that, too," one suggested. "Will you pray with us?"

Lynn explained the gospel again, questioned them, and then prayed with them. They also received Christ. Soon other Africans came and within thirty minutes a dozen people had accepted Christ. Lynn organized Ikulu Baptist Church out of that group, and it's still going strong more than twenty years later.

But the young man had more than a heart for missionary work. He also had a heart for the missionary's daughter. And she fell for him like a ton of the red, burnt bricks we make to build African churches.

Lynn was nine years older than our seventeen-year-old daughter, who was the same age and every bit as beautiful as Evelyn was when she captivated me. The same kind of overwhelming magnetism drew Lynn and Suzanne together. We worried about that powerful attraction and about the age difference, but the mature, spiritual way they handled their relationship earned our trust and admiration.

Evelyn and I had our first date on a New Year's Eve, and love sparked under the mistletoe. Lynn's and Suzanne's first official date came on a New Year's Day, when banana leaves likely took the place of mistletoe on an outing to see such natural wonders as the waterfall on the Kiwira River and *Daraja La Mungu* (God's Bridge), a magnificent natural bridge in the Tukuyu area.

Caught in a downpour which drove them under a banana tree for cover, they came home soaked, happy, and beginning to fall in love.

Finally, we stopped worrying and thanked God our daughter had someone as fine as Lynn Groce to replace the boyfriend she'd left behind in America, and everything else she'd given up, so her parents could answer the call to missions.

But some of the staff at Rift Valley Academy had a different reaction. When she came back to the campus from a month-long break in April and announced her engagement, it caused quite a stir. They'd never heard of such a thing at that mission boarding school.

Some of them even said she should be sent home,

but the ones with good sense prevailed. Suzanne finished and graduated from Rift Valley Academy in
1967, a very happy young lady.

Lynn attended her high school graduation, and
then they sadly parted for a year while we went on
furlough and he stayed to cover our work and finish
his Journeyman tour.

Suzanne completed a year of college and filled the
mail with letters to Africa during that long year
before Lynn returned to America. Jack Conley, a
missionary colleague, married them on August 3,
1968, at First Baptist Church, Tampa. Suzanne wore
the same gown Evelyn wore when we married in the
same church, in the same month twenty years earlier.

Then our family faced another wrenching depar-
ture, returning to the field with only eleven-year-old
Richard and two-year-old Edson, who was born in
Africa in 1966.

Walter stayed in the United States, at his own request, to finish high school and college at the North
Carolina School of the Arts, so he could prepare for
a career as a pianist.

Suzanne and Lynn headed off to Midwestern
Seminary to prepare for foreign missions. They returned to Africa about two years later as missionaries
to Ethiopia when Lynn was twenty-eight and Suzanne only nineteen. That's probably the first time in
modern history the Foreign Mission Board has allowed appointment of so young a missionary—and
more than likely the last.

Lynn's age, experience, and qualifications and Suzanne's Africa experience had something to do with the exception, but not everyone agreed with it.

During an unexpected lull in the crowd noise before their appointment service began, the wife of a Foreign Mission Board official was overhead to declare: "I *still* say she's too young."

The appointment service program had listed her as "nineteen and a half," but that hadn't fooled anyone.

Whether Suzanne was too young for appointment or not, it's remarkable how the exceptions on age that the board made for the Knapps—one for the father and two for the daughter—have led to long mission careers.

Lynn and Suzanne have worked in Ethiopia since 1969, with time out for furloughs and a year's work in Nairoibi during the height of a war with Somalia following the Marxist revolution which overthrew Emperor Haile Selassie.

Ironically, Bill Lewis, who so eloquently urged us to come to Tukuyu, urged Lynn and Suzanne to go to Ethiopia after he later transferred there. We wanted them to come to Tanzania, but God had other plans.

They and other missionaries to Ethiopia have had remarkable opportunities to make a spiritual impact there, before and during the devastating famine which drew the world's attention. That story rivals what happened among first-century Christians. Some day, when it's told, it will rank with the most exciting and productive stories in the history of Christian missions.

Meanwhile, Evelyn and I have our hearts in Ethiopia as well as in Tanzania. Lynn and Suzanne are rearing five of our grandchildren—Leslie, Douglas, Simon, Luke, and Crystal—in that ancient cradle of Ethiopian Orthodox (Coptic) Christianity.

Their firstborn, a thirteen-month-old baby girl, is buried in its soil.

5
Beyond the Mist

"Bwana Lewis, you haven't seen our new children."

A young man standing near the bamboo-and-banana-leaf Makwale Baptist Church building smiled at Bill Lewis and me.

"My wife has given birth to twins since you visited last," he said proudly.

He and other Africans loved Bill, who had pioneered mission work in the old Rungwe District of Tanzania. It later subdivided into three districts: Kyela District, where we now serve, Ileje, and the new Rungwe District.

The young man, a deacon at Makwale church, called his wife, and she brought two beautiful little brown babies over for us to see.

"We have a problem," he said, looking expectantly at Bill. "My wife doesn't always have enough mother's milk to feed these babies, and they get hungry and cry."

Bill had helped some mothers with powdered milk, but he couldn't help these two at the moment.

"I'm sorry," Bill answered regretfully. "We've run

out of the last of the milk, but we're expecting to get
some more in. Bwana Knapp or I will bring it to you
when I get some."

Evelyn had nursed children, so I added: "Tell your
wife to drink lots of water and eat beans and fish.
That'll increase her milk."

Bill and I had come the torturous fifty miles of
rutted dirt road down the mountain from Tukuyu,
where our two families then lived and worked, to
survey Makwale, a village in a valley at the foot of the
Livingstone Mountains.

We needed a site for a demonstration farm I would
establish. Maybe Makwale would be it.

Language school, and all its trauma, lay behind us
in distant Dar es Salaam, and we were into our first
term in late 1964 as "real, live missionaries" on what
our friends in Florida still thought of as the Dark
Continent.

Dar es Salaam, Tanzania's capital city, means "haven of peace." *Salaam* is the Arab version of the
Hebrew word *shalom.* The city had fascinated us as
we walked down its streets lined with small shops
where men cut and sewed leather for shoes, fash-
ioned material for suits, carved wood, or butchered
meat. We visited at least five different shops or markets to buy meat, vegetables, bread, and other items.
We had no supermarkets there—and still don't by
American standards.

In other ways, Dar es Salaam seemed modern with
its theaters, private social clubs, and beautiful hotels
lining the shore of the Indian Ocean. At least, it did

until we met lepers, with nubs for fingers and toes, begging on the post-office steps.

We'd experienced many African firsts in short order: a visit to a game park where wild animals roamed freely up to our car, a baptismal service on an early Sunday morning in the Indian Ocean, and new foods like East African curry, hippo and gazelle steak, warthog roast, *muhogo* (cooked cassava roots), and *samosas* (meat and onion deep fried in flour pastry).

The vagaries of driving British-style in the right side of the car on the left side of the road through the whirlwind traffic took a little while to master, but we learned. And we also learned not to leave our belongings on the car seat by an open window. Purse snatchers and thieves of all descriptions were commonplace in the downtown area.

Walter rode his bicycle almost everywhere, but he learned it was dangerous to run into someone in Africa. About thirty seconds after a minor bike accident one afternoon, a large crowd of angry Africans surrounded him ready to vent their pent-up anger on the white boy, who was wealthy by their standards.

But Walter's Indian friend, Lewis Pinto, saved the day by getting the crowd to let Walter go home and get his parents. We went to the police, and they dropped the matter after Walter made his statement. Angry crowds have been known to kill people who injure or kill someone in a traffic accident in Africa or other places in the Third World.

Lewis grew very close to our family during our

year of language study and became the first person we won to Christ in Africa.

Meanwhile, we struggled to learn Swahili, a trade language spoken throughout East Africa, mainly in Tanzania, Kenya, Uganda, and eastern Zaire. Arabs, who sailed down in their *dhows* to trade with Africans, devised it because every tribe in the Bantu group along the coast spoke a different language. So they took some words from one tribe and some from another, mixed them with some Arabic when they couldn't find a suitable Bantu word, and developed Swahili. It's about 25 percent Arabic, but also has a mixture of English, German, Portuguese, and some Gujarati (Indian) words which crept in through the years of colonial rule.

Supposedly, it's one of the easier African languages, but I found it plenty difficult. My family suffered through my early days of knowing enough for only one sermon, and I made more than my share of embarrassing mistakes long after we had left language school.

Even Evelyn, who caught onto Swahili more quickly in the beginning than I did, will never forget one of her most embarrassing moments with the language.

One day, quite awhile after we'd begun our agricultural ministry, one of our workers, a man named Mwakanusya, came to Evelyn, very agitated.

Mwakanusya spoke better Nyakyusa, the local tribal language, than he did Swahili. But he knew enough Swahili to talk to us. We spoke little or no Nyakyusa.

Evelyn had trouble understanding as he became more and more upset and one Swahili word tumbled over another. Finally, she figured out someone had died and then decided it must be his fiancée.

"Oh, *pole* (POH-lay)!" she exclaimed in the Swahili term of condolence. "How can I help you, Mwakanusya?"

"We need to take care of the body," he said, adding some other unintelligible comments.

Evelyn wanted to be helpful at such a sad time.

"Would you like to get the car and bring the body up here for burial?" she asked.

Mwakanusya looked at her in amazement, but he nodded.

"Yes, that would be fine, Mama Nepu."

She suggested he wait until I return so I could help make arrangements for a Christian funeral.

Mwakanusya looked at her even more strangely, but, in polite African manner, he agreed.

When I returned, Mwakanusya had calmed down and expressed himself more clearly. It was a mission cow *(ng'ombe)* that had died, not his fiancée *(mchumba)*.

He had been upset that the cow had died because he felt responsible for its care, and he'd come to ask if we wanted to save the meat. Some Africans will use the meat of an animal which has died of disease.

But they don't have funerals, Christian or otherwise, for dead cows. Mwakanusya must have thought white people were strange indeed.

As we struggled with Swahili in language school and then the formidable task of taking the *mtihani,* the government exam then required, we also stumbled over British English.

My face turned red when a local roof-repair *fundi* (expert) came over to patch a leak. He called down from the attic and asked for a "torch."

"A torch? Aren't you afraid of starting a fire up there?" I asked.

He exploded with laughter, and I quickly discovered he wanted a "flashlight."

Two shipments from the United States and a few sleepless nights transformed me into a *fundi* of sorts myself at getting things through the local docks and customs. When our first shipment arrived in Dar es Salaam, the largest crate was broken, from mishandling in Madagascar, and wide open for thieving fingers.

Since it had to sit out by the water's edge all night, I set up housekeeping beside it with a cot, thermos, and our faithful German Shepherd watchdog, Lassie. It was a little frightening on the dark wharf, but Lassie made the difference. The Africans wouldn't get near her, especially when her ears lay back, her nose wrinkled, her teeth glinted in the moonlight, and her low, steady growl said, "Scram, Bwana."

By noon the next day, everything had made it through customs and arrived at the house without even the loss of one agricultural pamphlet.

Finally, we faced a decision about where we would work. Tanzania, Uganda, and Kenya covered a lot of miles and had a lot of needs. The decision wasn't easy. The choice came after a forty-three-hundred-

mile *safari* in a Volkswagon Kombi through the *pori*
(wild country) of the three nations.

As the days went by on our trek, we experienced
a formal dinner by candlelight with zebra as the
main dish, traveled to church in a motorboat on Lake
Tanganyika—longest freshwater lake in the world—
and drove amidst herds of giraffe and elephants. We
saw warthogs darting across the road, vistas of gigan-
tic baobab trees as far as the eye could see, African
men carrying spears, women with huge loads on
their heads, naked Karamajong tribesmen, and the
sparkling water of Owen Falls in Uganda, one of the
sources of the Nile River.

Tanganyika united with Zanzibar under the name
Tanzania in 1964. About the size of Texas and New
Mexico, it's on the eastern side of Africa just south of
the equator and has more than twenty-one million
people and about 120 tribal groups. The country rises
from the coast, and then gradually increases in altitude as you go inland.

Most of Tanzania is a kind of high plateau with
several mountain ranges. As you drive north, you
approach the Usambara Mountains where the African violet originated. On toward the northwest, you
see Mount Kilimanjaro looming up on the boundary
between Tanzania and Kenya. Then, down to the
southwest of Dar es Salaam lie the Southern Highlands, made up of several mountain ranges.

The more we saw, the more we began to point
toward Rungwe District in the Southern Highlands
which gets 100 to 120 inches of rain a year. It had
great agricultural potential, and I was bursting to get

started. Elevations there range from fifteen-hundred feet to nine-thousand feet, and crops differ according to altitude: rice, bananas, and oranges in the lowlands; wheat, coffee, English peas, and various fruits in the highlands.

Finally, we made our decision, not because of Bill Lewis's persuasive visit back in Florida but because we felt God wanted us to work in Rungwe District and live in Tukuyu.

Now, we were settled in Tukuyu and had started the search for a site for the demonstration farm.

As Bill and I stood together in Makwale, admiring the young man's twins, some stark realties began to dawn on me. What would happen to these babies if the powdered milk didn't come in time?

Bill and I climbed into our Land Rover, planning to return as soon as possible with the milk.

Soon, the Lufirio River lay ahead, and we drove onto the "ferry"—fifty-five-gallon drums framed in with boards. Two perspiring Africans pulled us across. The river was impassible unless the level was right. If it got too high, the rushing water would wash the "ferry" away.

Not long after we got back to Tukuyu, the rainy season came, and two months passed before we could make it back to Makwale. Finally, the level dropped enough for me to chance a crossing, and I headed back—not certain at all whether we should build the new demonstration farm there—but I was determined to bring the powdered milk to the twins.

Despite my concern for the babies, the drive thrilled me as usual that day. Leaving Tukuyu behind, my Land Rover passed the giant Musekera and Chivanjee Tea Estates and the Ilima coal mine.

Finally, the road dropped to an infertile area of scrub, populated only by woodcutters who sell charcoal and firewood along the way. Then it entered the rich floodplain with a forest of banana trees, interspersed African fashion with plantings of pumpkins, beans, cassava, spinach, and taro root.

I turned left just a short way from Kyela, the principal village in the floodplain. It became the "county seat" in 1975 and now gives the district its name. The road led past thousands of acres of rice, the area's main crop. Here rice isn't hand planted in paddies but seed is directly broadcast on the prepared soil each December and January to await the flooding rains which inundate the fields.

Fortunately, the Land Rover had four-wheel drive because recent rains had also inundated the road.

I thought again of the twins as I nosed the Land Rover across a suspension bridge over the Mbaka River and then headed toward higher ground, featuring cashew trees, citrus, and later—cocoa.

The road wound its way through Ipinda, a poor little crossroads village with a few *dukas* (shops) and a rice mill. It crossed another floodplain and then approached the Lufirio River and its unique "ferry." Years later, a new steel bridge made the river passable the year around.

Beyond the ferry, the road degenerated into a cow trail that wouldn't become a gravel road until the 1980s. Clusters of grass huts, bananas, and citrus dotted the area, looking like a picture in my fourth-grade geography book.

Spatterings of rain thumped irregularly on the Land Rover's bonnet (hood) as I approached Makwale and wound my way through fifteen-foot-high elephant grass on either side of the trail in the sparsely populated area. Later, the area would become densely settled and almost entirely cultivated. But travel was a real adventure then.

Off to the northeast, the magnificent Livingstone Mountains, which form the eastern boundary of what is now the Kyela District, rose abruptly from the plain. In the distance they resembled a giant dinosaur's back. Slowing down, I surveyed the scene in awe, forgetting about everything but the beauty which surrounded me.

The grass gave way to large trees, and I proceeded cautiously as frightened Africans darted to safety at the sound of the car. They stood under the trees and stared as if Halley's Comet were passing. Vehicles and white people were rare in this isolated spot.

Suddenly, the spatterings turned to a downpour as the rainy season gave vent to its final fury. Rain pelted my windshield as I approached the little Makwale church, one of two Baptist churches then in that area. It slackened as I drove into the churchyard next to the thatched building.

Two little graves with bamboo crosses stood there starkly, accusingly. All was silent except for the pounding of my heart as I sat in the Land Rover and stared at the graves. Numbly, I got out of the car and searched for the twins' father.

"My wife got sick after the rains came, her *maziwa* (milk) dried up, and she couldn't nurse them," the young man said. "There was nothing we could feed them and not a single *ng'ombe* (cow) in the village at that time to give *maziwa*."

He paused and then continued sadly.

"We couldn't get out, and, finally, they just starved to death."

Tears stung my eyes as we stood quietly there together—one father hurting with another. Rain began to fall again, and thunder rolled down from the Livingstones and rumbled through the beautiful, needy valley.

An inner voice seemed to say: "These are My sheep. Feed them." At that moment, any doubt about the location of the demonstration farm vanished. It would be right here in this valley where these people had so much physical and spiritual hunger.

Inadequate roads and the remoteness of the location, about twenty-five miles from Kyela town, had caused serious doubts about Makwale as the site. But the more I investigated, the more I realized how much these people needed an agricultural ministry.

Over the years, our missionaries throughout the world have found that agriculturists—and specialists in such fields as veterinary medicine, appropriate technology, and community health—can make a big impact on world hunger. Southern Baptists had eighty-seven mission personnel in twenty-five countries assigned to agriculture in early 1986 alone, not including other specialists.

That kind of missions has special value in Africa—a troubled continent faced by drought, famine, and eroding economies. It helps people find a better way of life and creates opportunities to deal with spiritual needs. It expresses love and concern in a way people understand and appreciate and places missionaries in intimate, meaningful relationships with people.

Africa's not the only place it works. Take the Philippines, for example. Harold and Joyce Watson, a Southern Baptist missionary agriculturist couple appointed not long after Evelyn and I were, have made a great impact there. In 1985, Harold became one of only a handful of non-Asians to win the Ramon Magsaysay Award, considered in Asia as the equivalent of a Nobel Prize.

Harold was honored for helping "the poorest of small farmers" by encouraging international use of a hillside farming technique he and two Filipinos developed. They call it Sloping Agricultural Land Technology (SALT).

More than six-thousand people from Asian nations travel to the Philippines each year to study SALT, a program Harold believes can revolutionize the lives of three fourths of the families who farm in developing countries.

He summed up what I believe when he said: "It's not God's will that anyone suffer and go hungry. Christ came so that we could have abundant life. We're here to try somehow to help people have abundant life, physically and spiritually."

Harold's work has resulted in response to the the gospel message. From the beginning, Baptists have made evangelism and church development a strong part of their work at the Mindanao Baptist Rural Life Center, staffed by Harold, three other Southern Baptist agriculturists, fourteen Filipino agriculturists, and a Southern Baptist nurse team.

Another recent example is the Sanwabo Project in Burkina Faso, a West African country formerly called Upper Volta.

Baptists from Tennessee worked there in partnership with our missionaries and local Baptists to help more than eight-thousand people in seventeen drought-stricken villages.

Volunteers from America dug wells, built a dam and lake, gave literacy training, and helped with livestock, crops, and community health. The project radically changed people's lives and living conditions. It also changed their spiritual lives, as hundreds turned to Christ and churches began to spread because of related evangelistic efforts.

At a cemetery near the dam, the graves of most women are topped with the pots they used to carry miles to find water. The graves of most men are topped with their short-handled hoes.

Now they're beginning to be marked by crosses, an indication of the spreading Christian faith in an area where tribal worship and Islam dominate.

Norman and Beverly Coad, former Burkina Faso missionaries now transferred to the desperately needy country of Mali, said prayer broke the power that pagan beliefs held over the people of Burkina Faso. It set the stage for the spiritual breakthrough they needed more than water.

Evelyn and I also believe that prayer changes things, and we knew, as we began our efforts in Makwale in 1964, that we would need plenty of it to penetrate the area for Christ.

Witchcraft and things of *Usetani*, the Nyakyusa name for Satan or *Shetani*, god of the underworld, dominated their lives, enslaving them in fear and blinding them to the light of *Kyala*. Pagans included both *Kyala*, the Nyakyusa name for the one Creator God, and *Usetani* among the other gods and spirits they worshiped.

In a spiritual sense, even though early missionaries of other groups had established a foothold for Christianity, these people did live on a "dark" continent.

Much pagan influence has died out in recent years, but pagan Nyakyusa we found then believed they couldn't approach *Kyala* directly but must make sacrifices to placate their secondary gods of the forces of nature.

A lot of pagan religion was based on fear of witches and fear of death and funerals. They carried out pagan rites at funerals and insisted on burying people at night. Christians buried their dead during the daytime, but pagan family members usually came back at night, dug them up, performed rites, and reburied them.

They believed that the spirits of people remain nearby after death and gradually grow weaker and weaker as they are forgotten, finally disappearing into nothing. They made sacrifices of animals, beer, rice, chickens, or cows at shrines to commemorate ancestors and give them longer life in the spirit world.

During our years in Kyela District, we've seen much of paganism lose its grip on the lives of the people. The preaching of the gospel, along with the coming of such outside influences such as schools, radio, and the printed page, has weakened the influence of many old fears and superstitions. They often still hold sway at time of death, but their influence on daily life is much reduced. This change has left a vacuum which in recent years is being filled in many lives by a newfound faith in Christ.

Evelyn and I knew from the beginning that the situation in Kyela wouldn't be easy. But we knew we had to accept the challenge despite the difficulties. Early Christian missionaries, with none of the support and resources we had, made great sacrifices to do so. So did determined African Christians who had walked countless miles on bleeding, bare feet to bring Christ to distant corners of the bush.

Andelile, an old African man Bill Lewis had won to Christ, set that kind of example. He gave up several wives to become a Christian. Then he became a pastor and started a little church. After awhile, he grew concerned that his relatives—a whole clan of people up in the foothills of the Undali Mountains in the western part of Rungwe District—hadn't heard about Jesus.

The old man set out on foot to reach them, climbing the mountains barefooted to visit first one family and then another over a wide area. Eventually, twenty-one little churches dotted those mountains.

Bill, deeply moved by Andelile's dedication, wanted to help.

"What can I do for you, Andelile? Couldn't you use a bicycle?"

"Oh, no, Bwana Lewis, I don't know how to ride a bicycle. I'm too old for that. Besides, a bicycle wouldn't make it over those rocky trails."

Bill thought a donkey might work. His children had a pet donkey in the backyard which Andelile had seen.

Knowing his kids wouldn't like it, Bill offered Andelile the donkey because he felt a deep desire to help him.

"No, your children have spoiled the donkey, and he'd never let me ride him," the old man answered. "It wouldn't work."

"Well, what can I do?" asked Bill, who loved African pastors and would do all he could to help them.

The old man saw his friend cared for him and thought hard for awhile.

"You know, I think a pair of shoes would help a lot. So often my feet hurt. They get cut; they bleed and get sores."

Stunned by the wisdom and simplicity of the request, Bill got Andelile a pair of shoes.

Whenever we remember Andelile, Evelyn and I think of the Scripture verse which says, "How beautiful are the feet of them that preach the gospel of peace, and bring glad tidings of good things!" (Rom. 10:15).

We also remember that the original Baptist work

in Tukuyu started because of another African man: Anosisye Mwangwembe.

He trekked many miles barefoot over the Mporoto Mountains to Mbeya town three times in the late 1950s to tell newly arrived missionary Sammy De-Bord that God had told him Sammy must come and preach to his people.

Anosisye showed up one night at Sammy's door, and Sammy almost sent him away because he thought Anosisye was with a group which had come earlier wanting him to help them start a church for polygamists.

But Anosisye finally made Sammy understand he had journeyed from Tukuyu, across the mountain, to ask him to come and preach.

Sammy had often gazed at the mountains in the distance; the misty clouds which shrouded their peaks seemed to beckon to him to come on over. Now, he had a chance to go there, but he didn't think he had the time.

"I'm sorry," he told Anosisye. "I can't do it. I'm the only preacher missionary here, and I've got too much work."

Disappointed, Anosisye melted into the darkness.

A week later, Anosisye returned and pleaded with Sammy again. He had prayed for years that God would send a missionary to his people.

Sammy gave him the same answer, but this time he was deeply troubled. He made Anosisye's request a matter of daily prayer, and then one morning he told his wife, Teenie:

"I don't think I can say no again if Anosisye comes back."

That day, Anosisye returned for the third time over those many miles to beg for help. He was convinced God had answered his prayer by sending Sammy, and he wasn't about to give up.

True to his word, Sammy couldn't say no. Several days later, he loaded a portable organ into his Land Rover and headed toward the beckoning mist.

Anosisye met him along the way, and they drove for miles on the perilous, unpaved road before it ran out. Then they parked and labored several miles up the mountain on foot.

An eager group of worshipers awaited in a banana grove under a lean-to made of banana leaves especially for this service.

It took Sammy's breath away.

"It was the most beautiful temple I ever saw," he said later.

The mist had parted and opened up a new world for Southern Baptist missions. That banana leaf "temple" resulted in the Jerusalem Baptist Church and the beginning of new work in old Rungwe District.

That, in turn, became the launching ground for the startling evangelistic breakthroughs in recent years in Kyela District, a thousand-square-mile area carved out of old Rungwe District.

Sammy DeBord split time between Mbeya and Tukuyu until he and Teenie moved to Dar es Salaam. They took over the work there vacated by the famed East African missionaries Wimpy and Juanita Harper after Wimpy drowned in the Indian Ocean in 1958.

Missionaries Carlos and Myrtice Owens came to Mbeya and continued to work across the mountain until Bill and Nina Lewis moved there to live and work full-time.

Many other Southern Baptist missionaries besides the Lewises have passed through the mist to live in Tukuyu over the years. Besides Evelyn and me, they include Dale and Nelda Gann, Arville and Pauline Senter, Euclid and Janelle Moore, June Mason, Jack and Sally Conley, and Olan and Lynn Burrow.

Phil and Phyllis Washburn, appointed in late 1984, and Jon and Lisa Lord, appointed in late 1985, are assigned there now. They are our nearest missionary neighbors and the only Southern Baptist missionaries in Tukuyu. As many as four families have worked there together at a time, not including assorted short-term personnel.

About eighty Southern Baptist missionaries, with a variety of gifts and perspectives on missions, work in Tanzania today. They face a huge task in a country where economic conditions affect their ability to get the job done.

Oftentimes, a fuel crisis, which waxes and wanes in Tanzania with the availability of foreign exchange for outside purchases, will leave missionaries wondering from week to week whether they can get enough gasoline or diesel fuel for their wide range of ministries.

Some missionaries have had to curtail their work during those times or watch it grind to a halt, at least temporarily. Others manage to get enough fuel to maintain some semblance of normalcy.

Decreased mobility increases isolation of remote, single-family stations, such as ours, and can negatively impact church growth. For example, baptisms and new churches in thirteen of twenty-two associations of Baptist churches decreased or recorded no gain in 1983 in Tanzania because of lessened missionary mobility.

But increases in the other nine associations, including our Kyela District, caused a 1.8 percent overall increase in the number of churches and an 8.2 percent baptism gain in 1983. That was the lowest growth rate in years.

If missionaries don't come with a four-year supply of goods, they'll find themselves short of most of the necessities of life because local goods likely won't be available. Or, if they are, they sell for an inflated price such as forty dollars a gallon for cooking oil or fourteen dollars for a small box of laundry soap.

Gasoline, when it's available, costs sixty-five to one-hundred dollars per tankful. Transportation difficulties—compounded by bad roads, fuel problems, and scarce auto parts—could cause the Baptist Mission of Tanzania to rethink a philosophy of missions built on the concept of wide mobility.

"Even before this, we spent more than 50 percent of our time taking care of the logistics of living," one missionary said during a recent fuel crisis. "We sometimes wonder if it's worth our while to stay."

Some mission groups have decided cost and logistics aren't worth the effort, but Southern Baptists haven't reached that point.

Many of our missionaries have concluded that less

mobility may result in greater depth. Instead of far-flung ministries, we may have to invest ourselves more intensively with fewer people. Thousands of people live within motorcycle, bicycle, or walking distance of many mission stations in crowded Africa.

The more intense personal approach may be the way of the future in worldwide mission efforts as resources dwindle and dollars must stretch further and further.

We know from Evelyn's personal experience that a little bit can become a lot in God's arithmetic.

6
Evelyn's Story—Part One: God's Arithmetic

"Evelyn, is that you? What's wrong?"

Doug stood silhouetted in the doorway of our darkened living room in Makwale, straining to see.

Outside, all was quiet as moonlight filtered through the rain clouds which enveloped that wet December midnight in 1976. Inside, the only sound was my labored breathing.

Doug had just returned from a hard trip to Mbeya.

"Over here, Doug," I answered weakly. "I thought you'd never get here. I can barely breathe, and the pain is so terrible."

Doug hurried forward as I convulsed in another wave of pain in my right rib cage, and my breathing became more ragged. He winced as he looked into my haggard face and felt my forehead, but his gentle touch comforted me.

What a time to get sick!

We'd just returned from furlough to begin our fourth term in Tanzania with a new challenge in a new location—well, sort of a new location.

Just before furlough, we'd moved down the mountain from Tukuyu to live permanently on the farm in

Makwale and concentrate on Kyela District. No more commuting, as we'd done for ten years. Now we would really get down to business, especially among young people.

But how? Thousands of them lived in the area, and past efforts across the district had failed to bring them into our churches. We had to admit we hadn't figured out how to go about reaching them any better than other Baptists in East Africa at that time. Surveys showed Baptists mostly reached adults.

What a time to get sick!

"We've got to get you to Dr. Laffoon in Mbeya," Doug exclaimed, "but we can't leave until morning."

I groaned but understood. The rutted, precipitous, winding road from Makwale over the mountains to Mbeya would be treacherous at night anytime. Add the mud from the rainy season, and the trip could amount to suicide.

The night crept by. My pain intensified, and my breathing grew more shallow and ragged. Finally, as the dawn of December 16 painted the lush valley with streaks of pink, Doug loaded me and ten-year-old Edson into the Land Rover.

"Bye-e-e bye-e-e, Nepu," chanted African *watoto*, who scampered after the car, waving vigorously, their white teeth glistening from their dark faces.

As the children's farewell rang in my ears, I thought about our goals and wondered if God would allow us to return to fulfill them. Would I ever see Makwale again, or was this more of a good-bye than those children realized?

Doug looked stricken as the haunting "bye-e-e

bye-e-e" followed us down the road. Did he, too, wonder if this was the final good-bye?

Every bump on the rutted road jolted me during the unusually slow six-hour drive from Makwale to Mbeya to see missionary physician Bob Laffoon. He worked at the hospital Southern Baptists then operated there.

More than ten years earlier, another missionary physician, Dr. Ralph Bethea, had waited at the end of another journey, a painful two-hour trip from Tukuyu to Mbeya for Edson's birth on March 13, 1966.

I remembered how the rain pelted down that dreary March day and how huge potholes almost swallowed our little Volkswagon. Doug drove carefully to cushion our precious cargo, but the trip was rough.

Despite the rough trip and my age, then almost thirty-six, we delivered a healthy, nine-pound baby. But it was a painful delivery, much like the pain I now endured as we traveled to see Dr. Laffoon.

Dr. Laffoon's X rays showed I had such an enlarged liver that it had pushed against my right lung and caused it to fill with liquid.

He suspected an amoebic abscess of the liver and prescribed medication, but I showed no improvement.

Then the treatment got worse than the illness, at least psychologically. After I'd suffered for several days, Dr. Laffoon came to me on December 23 to explain his next step.

"Evelyn, I'm going to have to aspirate," he said.

That meant he would stick a long, deadly looking

needle through my rib cage in the back, with me sitting up and wide awake, to draw liquid from my lungs for examination.

Cringing inwardly, I remembered a vivid childhood experience in Silver City, a mining town in New Mexico. We had lived in primitive conditions in the remote area where my father worked as an electrical engineer for the government.

Mother came down with a severe case of tonsillitis, and the doctor's solution was to operate on her on our back porch, under a single, hanging light bulb with no anesthetic whatsoever!

She had simply opened her mouth, and the doctor had taken out her tonsils, inflicting terrible, terrible pain. That experience turned my father against doctors.

I didn't like Dr. Laffoon's needle, but I hadn't turned against doctors. He could do anything it took to end my pain.

But the test was inconclusive. Dr. Laffoon still couldn't diagnose the problem exactly, but he had some pretty grim-sounding opinions.

He gave me a shot to put me to sleep and then huddled with Doug. The sedative didn't put me under completely, and their conversation floated through my hazy senses.

"Doug, if I were you I'd take Evelyn to Nairobi immediately for further tests. Maybe the doctors in Kenya can find out what's really wrong," Dr. Laffoon advised.

"And then, personally, Doug, I think you'd better plan on going back to the States. She's either got cancer of the liver, advanced tuberculosis, or perhaps some complication with the amoebic abscess. I don't know why she doesn't respond. Something serious is wrong."

The sedation, though it didn't block out the conversation, created a surrealistic atmosphere.

"Bye-e-e, bye-e-e, Nepu" seemed to ring in my ears, like a call from the far end of a long corridor, and I thought back to the years of struggle to grow up, make it to the mission field, and launch our work.

I saw myself as a two-year-old perched on a plow in Lithia, Florida, while Daddy tilled the soil to survive after the Depression had wiped out our home and business.

When it got hot, I would drop my shoes between the furrows, and Mother would have to search the rows in the evening because we couldn't afford to buy another pair.

The voices of Doug and Bob Laffoon grew fuzzy. My eyes focused on my hand lying limply on the wrinkled bed linen, and I flashed back again, this time to Conchas Dam, New Mexico, about sixty miles north of Tucumcari, where Dad transferred to work on the construction of the huge, hydroelectric dam.

When I awoke on cold, winter mornings, I discovered little lines of snow had filtered through cracks in the bedroom wall to decorate my covers. I would lie there, dreading bare feet on a cold floor and a bare bottom in our cold outdoor toilet, while I smelled breakfast cooking on our kerosene stove.

The smell of food was luxurious. It was hard to find in those days, and hard to preserve because ice wasn't always available to cool our old-fashioned ice box.

Life in America's Depression in Florida and New Mexico had sure prepared me for Makwale with our remote location, renovated barn home, kerosene refrigerator, charcoal iron, wood stove, generator-powered lights at night, gravity-fed water system, and cooking from scratch.

Now all that, as well as all our plans for the future, lay in jeopardy as we prepared to leave Tanzania, perhaps for the last time.

Doug began immediately that night to make arrangements for the trip to Nairobi, praying he could get through by phone to book a flight. Americans, spoiled by the land of the instant dial tone, can reach out and touch someone anytime they wish. In Africa, phone connections, especially long-distance ones, are an adventure. It's a luxury to have a phone at all in the bush. We don't have one at Makwale.

A minor miracle happened. Doug got through on the first try to Missionary Aviation Fellowship in Dodoma, and MAF agreed to a Christmas Eve mercy flight to Nairobi the next morning at eight o'clock.

Then Doug and missionary Ray Blundell drove to Makwale to get all of our Christmas presents. They got back to Mbeya about 2:00 AM in time for Doug to grab a few hours sleep before the flight.

The African panorama sweeping beneath the small Cessna 185 the next morning would usually have fascinated me. Below, I glimpsed a wildebeest herd thundering across the plain. But I dropped my head back, too ill to enjoy the scene. Doug took me by the hand and began to pray silently.

The intensity of the prayer stood out in every line of his face. Over the years I'd learned that when Doug Knapp prays, things often happen. That thought comforted me tremendously.

Once, when a member of our family faced a severe crisis, Doug interrupted a long-needed vacation at the beach in Mombasa, Kenya, to fast and pray for three days. Things changed dramatically for the better in that person's life.

Another time, our Land Rover broke down in the bush and Doug couldn't fix it. Some people can't believe an agriculturalist isn't much of a mechanic. But that's the case with Doug.

Richard and I had walked ahead because we figured we'd get home before Doug could get the car started. We would get another vehicle and come back for him.

Doug prayed and then began to move his hands around under the hood.

"My hands sort of went to the water pump," he told me later. "I didn't even know it was a water pump at that time. I took it off, fiddled around with it, and then put it back on. The car started up right away."

That's a case of "celestial mechanics" if there ever was one!

But God hasn't always taken care of Doug's lack of mechanical aptitude or his absentmindedness: both have become legendary among his fellow missionaries.

His car broke down another time on a seldom-traveled back road from Masoko to Tukuyu. I guess if Snoopy from the "Peanuts" cartoon were to write that story, he'd begin, "It was a dark and cloudy night . . ."

That's exactly what it was—a totally dark night with the moon obscured behind heavy clouds.

The battery died about a mile from home. No amount of prayer got the Land Rover going, so Doug had to walk. But he'd forgotten to take a flashlight.

Not expecting prayer to make a flashlight material-ize in his hands, my husband felt his way hand over hand, crawling along the edge of the dark bush road. Every now and then, as he topped a rise, lights from the house gave him a landmark.

He made it home three hours later. I still shudder to think what creatures he avoided in the darkness. I guess God was taking care of Doug after all.

Now he always carries a flashlight, at least when he remembers to do it.

The hours of driving time down bush roads give Doug a special opportunity to pray. Thankfully, he does it with his eyes open and his hands on the wheel.

But some missionaries aren't so sure of that. Legend has it that a missionary found Doug stranded in a ditch along the road.

"I forgot I was driving and ended up in the ditch," Doug reportedly said.

That's bound to be a legend which has grown up in East Africa's Knapp lore. Doug can't remember it. And he's not *that* absentminded.

Missionary Jack Conley has kidded that Doug has a special guardian angel to keep him alive in Africa. Everyone needs a guardian angel to avoid the pitfalls of Africa. Maybe Doug's angel works just a little harder than others to keep the path clear for this sensitive, single-minded man who dreams dreams of spiritual revival in Tanzania, and then sees them come true.

Besides spiritual revival, Doug also prays for the physical needs of the people and spends a great deal of himself to help them—some believe too much.

Right or wrong, he works hard at missions and has both the results and the ulcers to prove it.

As our Cessna hurried on toward Nairobi, I tried to forget my pain by thinking back on our life together.

I thought about Doug's empathy for people. Because they mean everything to him, he will minister by the hour to the needs of Africans who line up at our door, while dinner grows cold on the table. That was hard to get used to, but I finally decided if I was going to live with Doug Knapp—which I most certainly was going to do—I would have to learn to understand him.

A key to understanding him is to realize he's a planner, a thinker, a dreamer, and a man who has the gift of compassion like no one I've ever known.

He's put so much emphasis on physical assistance, especially clothing for ragged Africans, that it has created misunderstandings. Some missionaries think Doug has done too much and say it creates problems for them when Africans they work with want them to do the same thing.

Left: Doug Knapp, age seven, with his pet guinea pig (ca. 1934)

Above: Evelyn Brizzi with her third-grade teacher in New Mexico (1939)

Above: Doug and Evelyn beginning their odyssey together

Right: Evelyn and Doug shortly after entering the seminary (1963)

The Knapps on a camping trip before leaving for Africa—Suzanne and Walter in the rear and Richard in the front

Suzanne and Walter, ages five and three (Don Ray Studios Photo, Tampa, FL)

Suzanne and her husband, V. Lynn Groce, upon their appointment as missionaries to Ethiopia—1969 (Foreign Mission Board Photo by Lawrence R. Snedden)

Near Tukuyu, Evelyn Knapp teaching the Bible to Hobokela Angetile and Salaya Filimon, leaders in WMS (FMB Photo by Gerald S. Harvey)

Doug preaching at an outdoor service near Tukuyu (FMB Photo by Gerald S. Harvey)

Doug passing out seeds for people to plant in their gardens—locale: the Makwale Baptist Demonstration Farm (FMB Photo by Gerald S. Harvey)

At Kapolwe Baptist Church, Doug helping Sunday School children tend their gardens—the children sold their vegetables to buy a Bible and Bible story book (FMB Photo by Gerald S. Harvey)

On the Tala Tala Baptist Church field, Doug and a helper preparing a seed bed (1966)—(FMB Photo by H. Cornell Goerner)

The pastor of Kapolwe Baptist Church, Thomson Mwakasisye, and Doug looking at a soybean crop (FMB Photo by Gerald S. Harvey)

Doug showing pineapples to a group of farmers at Makwale (FMB Photo by Gerald S. Harvey)

Doug with Ayrshire cattle amid Stera and Rhodes grass (FMB Photo by Gerald S. Harvey)

In the same area Doug explaining the preparation and value of vegetables (FMB Photo by Gerald S. Harvey)

Lynn and Suzanne Groce, with their sons, Douglas, Luke, Leslie, and Simon, are sharing an Ethiopian dish, injera. A fifth child, Crystal, is not shown. Their first child, Joylene, died in Ethiopia. The Groces have played a major role in combating hunger (Foreign Mission Board Photo by Joanna Pinneo)

Robert O'Brien, center, offers greetings to a newly-forming church in Malawi, across the Songwe River from the Kyela District of Tanzania. Evelyn Knapp is on the right and a Malawian translator on the left (FMB Photo by Joanna Pinneo).

Two men pole a dugout canoe as dusk deepens on storied Lake Nyasa, a 360-mile-long body of water to the south of the Kyela District (FMB Photo by Joanna Pinneo).

A recent shot of Doug demonstrating agricultural techniques at a "field day" in a village of the Kyela District (FMB Photo by Joanna Pinneo)

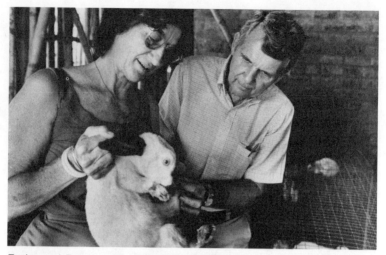

Evelyn and Doug tending to a rabbit on their Baptist Demonstration Farm in Makwale (FMB Photo by Joanna Pinneo)

The Knapps and Tanzanian workers feeding pigs on the Demonstration Farm (FMB Photo by Joanna Pinneo)

Doug talking with a tractor driver on the Demonstration Farm, which provides plowing services for the area (FMB Photo by Joanna Pinneo)

Doug preaching in the Kyela District (FMB Photo by Joanna Pinneo)

Doug encouraging those who have made decisions for Christ (FMB Photo by Joanna Pinneo)

Doug in conversation with a community leader (FMB Photo by Joanna Pinneo)

The Knapps crossing the Songwe River from Tanzania to Malawi for preaching services and baptism at new work started by Simoni Mwambobe (FMB Photo by Joanna Pinneo)

Doug baptizing in the Songwe River as Simoni Mwambobe baptizes in the background (FMB Photo by Joanna Pinneo)

Evelyn in the pantry of their home on the Baptist Demonstration Farm—Tanzanian missionaries must bring four years of supplies to make it through a term (FMB Photo by Joanna Pinneo).

The Knapps help themselves to chicken, rice, and beans cooked by Tanzanians in honor of their visit to a bush church (FMB Photo by Joanna Pinneo).

Evelyn carries on extensive work among young people and women throughout the district. Here she discusses the progress of the work with leaders (FMB Photo by Joanna Pinneo).

Tanzanian pastor Benjamin Panza teaches students about God in a bush school, Kyela District (FMB Photo by Joanna Pinneo).

Evelyn's work with youth has resulted in a Tanzania-wide youth organization. Here young people are in the middle of Bible Sword Drills (FMB Photo by Joanna Pinneo).

Left: Doug sharing the glorious good news of Jesus Christ (FMB Photo by Joanna Pinneo)

Above: This young man, Bible in hand and singing praises to God, sums up the whole story! (FMB Photo by Joanna Pinneo).

Doug understands that. "If I've erred, it's been on the side of doing as much as I can for people," he admits. "When I see Africans with clothing so ragged it won't cover their nakedness, I think about what the Bible says about clothing the naked, and I remember how desperately ashamed I was to wear revealing clothes to school and church in the Depression in Florida. I'll never forget the thoughtful people who understood that and helped me."

But differences of opinion and philosophy aren't bad. One shouldn't expect all missionaries to agree. We don't. Missionaries have strong opinions, beliefs, and philosophies of missions. The mission field attracts many leaders and few wishy-washy followers. It takes drive and determination to get here and survive here.

Consensus doesn't exist on many philosophies of missions, especially on how to help poor people. Missionaries who work in Third World countries, especially where things are scarce, face a dilemma from the day they arrive on the field in knowing how far to go in helping nationals physically.

We only have so much time, energy, and resources, but Africans usually don't understand that. By African standards, all white people, including missionaries, are rich. As citizens of the developed world, we have more things to dispose of than most of them ever dream of owning.

Missionaries don't want to give so much it makes Africans dependent or willing to profess Christianity for material gain. We don't want to give so little they feel we don't have the love of Jesus Christ.

African culture doesn't sharply divide the physical and spiritual dimensions of life, as we do in the Western world. For Africans, all things have spiritual dimensions, as any agriculturist who tries to change their farming or health habits quickly learns.

When Africans have a physical need, they also see it as a spiritual problem, much like the ancient Hebrews did. Therefore, when Africans perceive someone as stingy, they translate it in their own minds as unspiritual and unloving.

Some Africans may think some missionaries err on the side of doing too little. Whether they do or not, it's not because missionaries don't love people. They're either trying hard not to make people overly dependent, or they don't have the time and access to the resources for widespread physical assistance.

That's not the only philosophical dilemma missionaries face. Another one involves financial support.

For example, Doug's evangelistic work over the years has attracted the attention of people in the United States who want to give over and above their tithes to help. This creates the dilemma of how to receive it with integrity.

Missionaries, supported by our Cooperative Program unified budget and Lottie Moon Christmas Offering, aren't permitted to promote special gifts.

But missionaries can tell what they need when people ask and then accept the help they offer. That assistance is valuable as mission dollars must stretch further and further, but it shouldn't be given at the expense of our main support channels. And it can create gray areas of interpretation.

Add that to the long list of subjects which cause differences of opinion among missionaries.

That list was too long for me to contemplate as my pain intensified in our small, bouncing aircraft.

Thankfully, the trip was almost over. The plane's radio began to crackle with landing instructions as we approached Nairobi.

Missionary physician John Adams waited at Wilson Airport to take us to Nairobi Hospital for an appointment with Dr. Bagshaw, who was very British and a very good diagnostician.

"Cancer is a possibility, Mrs. Knapp," Dr. Bagshaw said in her clipped British way after a thorough examination.

"But I do believe your Dr. Laffoon was correct about the amoebic abscess of the liver. I shall treat you for that and see what happens."

With that she prescribed medication and left for a four-day Christmas vacation.

Christmas Eve in a hospital doesn't sound desirable—and it isn't—but it turned out to be the most unusual and spiritual Christmas I've ever experienced.

Voices singing the old classical Christmas carols in English wafted up and down the halls as Doug, Edson, and I held onto each other, thanked God for the safe trip to Nairobi, and committed ourselves to Him.

Visiting hours drew to a close, and Doug bent to kiss me good night as he and Edson prepared to leave for a room they had found at the Methodist guest house.

A pert Kenyan sister (nurse), her little white cap

cocked high on her Afro, stopped in the door. Clutching a tray of medication self-consciously, she back pedaled out the door, her dark skin concealing a blush.

I smiled inwardly, remembering how Tanzanians had responded in the beginning to our displays of affection.

Nyakyusa men and women, like most Africans, show little affection or closeness in public or at home, a fact of the culture which creates barriers between them. The male-dominated, polygamous culture doesn't help the situation much.

Over the years, Doug and I have tried to model a Christian marriage, including normal displays of affection. At first, Africans watched with amazement. Then men who admire Doug tried showing the same tenderness and concern for their wives, and it revolutionized their marriages.

I've also counseled wives on how to create an atmosphere which will break down barriers. They respond because no one wants the loneliness that strained relationships create.

Once, when Doug was getting ready to travel, I kissed him good-bye. Some African men were watching through the living room window, and another missionary heard one say: "If my wife would kiss me good-bye like that, I'd leave more often."

I didn't want to think about any kind of good-bye as I lay in my hospital bed in Nairobi, wondering what the future held. I certainly didn't want Doug and Edson to leave. But they did, and I settled down to try to sleep.

But between the pain and the treatment, I got little sleep after they left for the Methodist guest house. Nurses took my blood pressure every fifteen minutes until after midnight the first night to make sure I could handle the powerful injections Dr. Bagshaw had prescribed. Thankfully, I could.

Doug and Edson returned the next morning with the presents Doug and Ray Blundell had salvaged from Makwale, and we celebrated Christmas in the hospital room.

The nurses put up a tiny, little Christmas tree and ordered a meal for Doug and Edson, so I wouldn't have to eat Christmas dinner alone. Then missionaries in Nairobi who had heard I was there began arriving to bring gifts and good wishes.

All that was wonderful, but I'll never forget what happened that afternoon after everyone had left. Alone in my room, I began reading through Psalms and suddenly riveted in on Psalm 103.

> Bless the Lord, O my soul: and all that is within me, bless his holy name.
> Bless the Lord, O my soul, and forget not all his benefits:
> Who forgiveth all thine iniquities; who healeth all thy diseases;
> Who redeemeth thy life from destruction;
> Who crowneth thee with lovingkindness and tender mercies;
> Who satisfieth thy mouth with good things; so that thy youth is renewed like the eagle's (1-5).

Those verses overwhelmed me, and I read all

twenty-two verses and committed them to memory as I lay in the bed. God's love enveloped me as I remembered all He had done in our lives.

I prayed:

"Lord, if it's time for me to go and be with You, that's all right. I understand, and I'm ready. But Lord, if it can be Your will to heal me, I wish that I could finish the job of being Edson's mother, bringing him up, and raising him."

Memory of that day still brings tears to my eyes because it was a very emotional experience. It also fills me with wonder.

Three days later, Dr. Bagshaw had the same reaction.

She poked and she listened, frowned, and then poked and listened some more.

My heart leaped. What had she found?

She poked and listened some more, and then looked up, slowly tapping her stethoscope in the palm of her hand.

"Well, Mrs. Knapp, you've made a remarkable improvement. I usually . . ."

She stopped, as if not believing what she'd found, and poked and listened again.

Then she cleared her throat and began again.

"I don't usually believe in miracles, but . . ."

Again, she didn't finish the sentence, but I got the message.

God had healed me. Tests showed my liver was almost back to normal size. I could breathe freely, and I had no more pain.

Dr. Bagshaw dismissed me from the hospital the

next day but kept me in Nairobi for several weeks. She still couldn't believe I was recovering.

Finally, she said I could return to Makwale, but she sent me off with these parting words: "Mrs. Knapp, you are not to drive over any bumpy roads in a four-wheel-drive vehicle for the next six months."

That was like being condemned to jail in Makwale. We then had nothing but a four-wheel-drive Land Rover—and nothing but bumpy roads.

But it didn't take long for me to realize Dr. Bagshaw knew what she was talking about. I hurt a lot every time I disobeyed and went out to churches with Doug across Kyela District.

For some reason, God had slowed down the healing process. I began to get impatient because we had plans and goals, such as reaching all those young people.

I couldn't understand the delay, but I finally did understand I had to slow down or suffer the consequences.

That's when I rediscovered the little Makwale Baptist Church, right there on the farm in walking distance. That would be my church for six months, so I decided to make good use of my time there.

I found just a handful of young people there, with no literature, no Sunday School, no teachers, and no one to notice they were alive. They would just come awhile, sing and pray together, and wait for church to start.

And we wondered why Baptists couldn't reach young people! At least I could help them until I was well.

The pastor was enthusiastic when I asked his permission to start a Sunday School.

"Oh, yes! That's wonderful! You are our missionary. You do anything you want to."

He didn't ask why his missionary, who lived a half mile away, had taken so long to notice the need.

Within a short time, I had a good crowd. Young people everywhere respond when someone cares.

I began to get excited and said, "Let's study the Bible."

They brought me back to earth.

"We don't have any Bibles, Mama Nepu."

So I gave them a sheetful of Bible verses to memorize and promised to give Bibles to those who learned them all.

I thought it would take a long time, but a week later a young man named Diki Gidioni came to me and said, "Mama Nepu, I'm ready to quote my Scripture for you."

"That's good, Diki," I said, expecting him to recite one or two verses.

But no, he had the whole thing memorized from start to finish. Fortunately, I had a Bible to give him.

Then, after several of them had earned Bibles, I realized they needed to learn more about the Bible.

"Let's turn to Genesis, the twelfth chapter," I said one Sunday morning.

"Oh, Mama Nepu, what page is that on?"

They didn't even know Genesis is the first book in the Bible. So we began learning the books, memorizing them and singing them in a Swahili song. That lead to teaching them the old-fashioned Bible Sword

Drills, which train students to find references quickly.

The young people loved it and began studying at home and practicing. Soon they located Bible verses with lightning speed.

The more they learned, the more they wanted to learn. Soon many began to accept Christ and take an active role in the church.

African pastors in the Kyela District heard something was happening at Makwale and many of them came to see for themselves. They were amazed. They'd never seen young people do anything like this.

"Mama Nepu," they pleaded, "won't you come and teach our young people, too?"

But I was still grounded.

I did the next best thing—which turned out to be the best thing I could have done—train an African to reach other Africans.

I put Diki Gidioni on a bicycle and sent him to the other side of the district to set up a youth program at another church. I tied a huge stalk of green plantains (cooking bananas) on the back of the bicycle so he wouldn't have to take too much time out, Tanzanian style, from teaching to earn his food.

Tanzanians are generous and hospitable. If you visit for three days, they'll feed you, but on the fourth day they expect you to get out on the *shamba* to help earn your keep. A Swahili proverb literally means what it says: "Three days for food and the fourth day, a hoe."

Diki didn't stay just four days. He stayed three weeks and taught them what he'd been taught.

After that, Diki traveled on his bicycle from church to church, starting so many youth programs they called him "the father of youth work" in Tanzania. I guess that makes me the grandmother.

Today, we have more than two-thousand young people in strong youth programs in most of the 250 churches in Kyela District. Doug says the youth movement has helped him and African evangelists lay the groundwork for the spiritual breakthroughs in Kyela since 1976.

The youth program has had several other results:

—It has spilled over the borders of the Kyela District and sparked a Tanzania-wide youth organization. Diki was its first chairman.

—It has affected and will continue to affect Tanzanian family life. After twenty years here, we could count on two hands the number of Christian marriages we'd had. Most have been young people from our youth program in the last several years who've gotten old enough to marry.

—It's also created a reservoir of young people ready to serve where they're needed in Kyela District churches or in a national thrust in home missions, which we've just begun to visualize.

Pastors who need church leaders look first among the older young people who have been through the youth program. Many of them have become pastors themselves.

—Most importantly for me, it taught me a lesson

about what can result when you slow down and observe.

I had to get sick to learn that running in wide circles doesn't always achieve our grand designs. Often a little concentrated effort close to home can produce the greatest results.

Truly, in God's arithmetic, a little bit often does become a lot.

7
Evelyn's Story—Part Two: The Edge of Discovery

Our Land Rover gave a gurgle—more like a death rattle—and died right there in the mud.

Doug, ever the optimist, tried to coax enough power from the sickly battery to get it started, but it only whirred futilely.

There we sat with a car full of African passengers, ready for another one of our "delightful" outings in a disabled vehicle on a bush road in Tanzania.

"It's no use, Evelyn," Doug muttered in disgust. "It won't start. We'll have to push it off again."

"Oh, no! That's all we need," I exclaimed, with undisguised chagrin.

Suddenly, the whirring grew louder, and I looked outside in delight. Maybe we wouldn't have to get out there in the mud and push after all.

But then I wished I hadn't looked.

A swarm of deadly bees—hundreds and hundreds of them—had descended on our car.

I've never seen people close windows so quickly. We should have applied for a new category in the *Guinness Book of World Records* for "fastest window closing in a killer bee onslaught." We may have moved even faster than our son Richard, who could have had a record of his own for "fastest automobile jack lowering in an elephant stampede" after an earlier narrow escape.

Right then, though, our minds were on windows, not on world records. We had a problem. We'd forgotten about the left rear window.

There wasn't one.

As the deadly swarm covered every surface of the car like a blanket, Roida Benjamin, a pastor's wife, jerked off her cloth *kanga* and held it over the gap.

Relieved, we expelled the breath we'd held, and then quickly sucked it right back in again.

The bees, which had settled all over the cloth, began creeping in around the edges and stinging Roida's fingers through the fabric.

We knew of cases in Africa where tied up cows had died of repeated stings and other cases where people trapped in cars had been hospitalized in critical condition.

"Quick, let's make a run for that hut over there," Doug shouted. "It's our only chance."

Hiking our jackets up over our heads, we made a what you might call a beeline for the thatched hut.

Someone once wisely advised, "Don't look back. Something might be gaining on you."

We didn't have to look back to know that something was not only gaining on us but finishing in a dead heat with us as we burst through the door of the hut.

An African man and his wife, seated in front of a small fire, dropped their bowls of *ugali* and jumped

up, startled, as we invaded their home without ex-
changing the traditional, polite *"Hodi?"* ("May I
come in?") and welcoming *"Karibu."*

They caught on quickly and forgave our breach of
etiquette.

"Nyuki! Nyuki!" the man exclaimed in instant
recognition of the bees.

His wife, a woman of few words, lept into action
against the *nyuki.* Smoke swirled up, filling the hut,
as she threw dried banana leaves on the fire. She'd
been through this drill before.

I slapped at the *nyuki* stinging my neck, wrists,
and hands as we waited for the smoke to drive them
away.

It did just that, but it made them madder than
hornets. Bees madder than hornets are a sight to
behold. They circled outside in a dark, undulating,
buzzing cloud.

After awhile, Diki Gidioni, one of our passengers,
courageously seized an opportunity when the *nyuki*
were briefly distracted to slip through enemy lines,
under cover of blanket. He planned to borrow a bicycle down the road and go after a can of powerful
insecticide spray we had at the farm.

The rest of us stayed put, reasoning that too many
moving targets would lead to another attack.

In the meantime, Diana Mwakasisi, another of our
African friends, hit upon a plan.

Diana believes she has extra courage and extra
protection because she's given birth to twins. Many
Africans traditionally see twins as an evil omen, but
not Diana.

She wrapped herself in a blanket, took a pan full of smoking leaves, dashed outside, and put it in the back of the Land Rover where many bees swarmed.

All it did was drive them to the front of the Land Rover—and make them madder: we were no better off than before.

We waited, fretting and coughing in the smoke, for an hour until Diki returned armed with the insecticide. He blasted his way through the swarm and dropped, panting, in the hut.

Gentle, mild-mannered Benjamin Panja, one of the African pastors, then took his turn at distinguishing himself in combat. He wrapped up in a blanket and launched a one-man charge, with fear and trembling, against the Land Rover stronghold, firing volleys of insecticide as he zigzagged through the dive-bombing enemy.

The bees, not outmanned but certainly outgunned, dropped like flies; then they fled in disarray. We fled, too, after pushing and straining through ankle-deep mud to get the cranky Land Rover going again.

Life everywhere has its share of unusual occurrences. Somehow, they seem bigger and more exaggerated in a distant land.

The African bush, out beyond the urban shield, generates its own brand of legends—with killer bees, wild animals, untamed terrain, and exotic-sounding but serious diseases such as elephantiasis, kwashiorkor, cholera, malaria, and bilharziasis (schistosomiasis).

Over the years, African life has taught Doug and

me how important prayer and God's protection are
as we've crisscrossed this unpredictable bush country.

The episode which really proved that to us happened some twenty years ago during our first term
as missionaries on an horrendous four-day trip from
Tukuyu to Nairobi.

A young African woman named Ndymake and our
four children, ranging from sixteen years old to four
months, accompanied us on the trip to attend the
annual meeting of the Baptist Mission of East Africa.
That was before the mission divided into the Baptist
Missions of Tanzania, Kenya, and Uganda.

Ndymake went along to take care of four-month-
old Edson while I attended the sessions. We didn't
have nurseries there.

The first day, we planned to go from Tukuyu to
Iringa, Tanzania, and spend the night.

Fifteen-year-old Walter didn't last that long.

"I don't feel very good, mother," he complained as
we bounced along the rough road. "I'm hot, and I
have a terrible headache."

That night we gave him antimalarials, the first line
of defense most bush missionaries use against that
type of symptom.

The next day, on a short but hard grind through
mountains to Dodoma, Walter got much worse. The
medicine hadn't helped, and we were really concerned.

After an overnight stop at Dodoma, we made a
mat for Walter in the back of the Land Rover and
pushed on since Dodoma had no doctors at that time.

Eight grueling hours later we arrived in Arusha, Tanzania, exhausted and extremely concerned about Walter.

Mary Saunders, then a missionary nurse there, took us immediately to a small, four-bed clinic run by a German doctor.

"This boy has typhoid fever!" the doctor exclaimed after a short examination. "You vill have to leave him here tonight, and the rest of you vill need inoculations," he explained in his thick German accent.

He suggested Edson also have his DPT shot, which Mary agreed to give him. Poor baby. In just four months of life, he'd already been exposed to typhoid fever and smallpox.

After his birth in Mbeya, we took him home to Tukuyu when he was just a few weeks old. An African baby, whose father had visited our home, died of smallpox soon after our return.

I was terribly frightened, and we rushed Edson back to Dr. Ralph Bethea in Mbeya. Dr. Bethea vaccinated him at an unusually early age.

Now we faced the spectre of illness again. With some misgivings, but realizing it was the right thing to do, we left Walter at the German doctor's clinic about 7:00 PM and went with Mary.

But the evening had only begun. About thirty minutes after Mary injected Edson, he started screaming, crying, wailing, and bawling. He'd had a bad reaction to the DPT.

My head reeled, and I wondered what could go wrong next. I didn't have to wait long to find out.

Suzanne said, "Mother, I feel so sick. I've got a fever."

She was sixteen years old and recognized her condition. So did I. She was breaking out with measles.

"Mother," nine-year-old Richard chimed in, "I've got little red spots all over me, too."

So there we were. Richard and Suzanne were in bed with measles. The baby was screaming his head off. Walter was in the clinic somewhere with typhoid fever attended by a doctor I'd never seen before, and I didn't know whether he would live or die.

I wanted to cry, but was interrupted by a knock at the door.

There stood Ndymake, the young woman we'd brought to care for Edson at mission meeting. We thought she was staying with African friends who worked at the Baptist seminary in Arusha.

Ndymake was in a frenzied state, talking rapidly and almost incoherently about someone chasing her and bothering her. We brought her into the house and tried in vain to calm her down. We called Davis Saunders, then president of the seminary, and he tried to console her in his usually calming way.

But nothing worked. She rattled on about people snatching at her clothes and trying to pull her hair. Suddenly, she jumped up and ran out the door, shouting at the top of her lungs.

Davis and Doug chased her down, struggled to get her into a car, and took her to a larger district hospital in town where they put her in a straightjacket.

Doug finally got back, and we went to bed about 2:00 AM after the baby had quieted down.

I trembled as we lay there, too tense to sleep. Something terrible had gone wrong.

"Honey, what in the world has happened to us?" I asked as Doug put a comforting arm around me.

"Well, I've thought about it," Doug replied slowly. "This is August, the month of vacations back home, and I guess people have forgotten to pray for missionaries. We've just been left out here without prayer."

That impressed me and has stuck with me over the years. Prayer support is important to missionaries on the field. Without it, we're open to attack.

The next day, things began to improve. Edson recovered within twenty-four hours. Suzanne and Richard turned out to have mild, ordinary cases of measles. Walter also began to get better. But we continued to pray fervently for Ndymake who showed no improvement.

Within a week we went on to Nairobi with all the children but without Ndymake. We still didn't know what was wrong with her.

Doug attended most of the mission meeting, but I could only go once or twice because of the baby and Walter's visits to the hospital to take a series of further tests.

About three weeks later, we returned through Arusha and found that Ndymake had recovered. She'd contracted cerebral malaria, a rare variety of the disease which affects the brain. It can kill or do permanent mental damage, but Ndymake suffered no long-lasting effects.

She doesn't remember any of the gory details of that night, but I sure do. I'll never forget that horrible, horrible night in Arusha and what it taught us about the value of prayer.

Athletes, realizing the value of the breaks of the game, have quipped that if they had to choose they would rather be lucky than good.

Doug and I have a variation on that. We'd rather have God's strength, wisdom, and guidance than all the worldly knowledge and expertise humans can muster. We want to undergird everything we do with prayer.

Missionary pilot Cordell Akin feels the same way. He's a veteran missionary and experienced pilot with a lot of knowledge and expertise, but he puts first things first. Cordell begins every flight of Baptist Air, the Baptist Mission of Tanzania's aviation service, with prayer.

That's proved its value more than once, most recently on a trip from Nairobi to Mbeya with three passengers: me and two Tanzanian Baptists, Jaston Binala and Osten Mwakijungu.

We were about a hundred miles out of Nairobi when oil began to spatter all over the windshield of the Cessna 210, one of two small Baptist Air planes flown by Cordell and missionary Bill Stiles. Nothing lay below but the bush country around Namanga, Kenya, near the Tanzania border, populated by wild animals and the cow-herding Masai tribe.

Cordell flew low over a potential landing site to drive off impala and wildebeest which covered the area. Then he made two more passes to try to examine the field, despite extremely poor visibility through the oil-streaked windshield. He landed successfully on his fourth approach.

We had little time to count our blessings. Masai came running from nearby huts, fascinated by the plane and by the white passengers. They milled around, touching my skin and hair in amazement.

One of the men carried a long, deadly spear which Masai *moran* (warriors) have used down through the years to distinguish themselves in combat against lions and in wars with other tribes.

We had no reason to fear the spear. The Masai don't go to war anymore, but they still can take care of themselves in the bush.

I was very glad to have them around because lions roamed freely in the area. In fact, Kenya missionaries Carl and Gerry Hall, who work in the Namanga area, have fenced in their home to keep lions and elephants out.

The Halls live so far out it takes an experienced tracker to find them without directions. Once they wrote out directions for a visit by Robert and Shirley O'Brien, who then lived in Nairobi, which showed how remote their location is. After the O'Briens and their sons, Eric and Paul, turned off the paved road from Nairobi, they followed these directions:

"Turn right just past the large, dry riverbed at Mili Tisa. After about a quarter of a mile, just after passing a school on the left, turn left at the old Arusha track.

"Follow the dirt track about a mile past one bridge," the directions continued. "Then turn right at the giraffe thigh bone. After about two miles, the track forks at a large anthill."

The Halls meant a *large* anthill. The small insects, more like flying termites, build hills sometimes twice as tall as people. There's no way you can miss one. We have the same kind of thing in Tanzania.

Many Africans consider the insects a delicacy and will grab them on the wing and eat them like candy. To my horror, Richard and Edson tried that, too, when they were growing up.

"Take the right fork at the anthill," the Halls's directions continued. "About a mile further on you'll enter an area of large trees. There you'll find an 'intersection' in the track. Turn right.

"You'll see a low-hanging dead limb, and then it looks like the road ends. It doesn't. It's just a low-water bridge for crossing the river. Cross there.

"Immediately after coming up the bank, you'll see our fence on the right. Just follow the track to our gate. Welcome to the Hall house!"

The O'Briens pulled up to the gate, thankful just to find the place and glad the welcome mat wasn't out for some other visitors who had left their "calling card"—lion paw prints—in the dust there.

The Hall house, which Carl and Gerry built from the ground up while they camped in the wilds, has become a focal point for effective ministry in the area.

Baptist work began there in 1977 with a community development project and church development emphasis. It took awhile for Carl and Gerry to make a spiritual impact because the Masai are fiercely independent and extremely oriented to their own group.

Missionary Harold Cummins, who made a dramatic breakthrough among Masai in another part of Kenya after a long period, says that when a Masai makes a decision for Christ, it's a "multi-individual decision."

In 1983, Harold baptized a century-old Masai, Kiriswa Nairrotiai, known as the "killer of many lions." When the old lion killer, who was in his twenties a year before Nairobi was built in 1899, "put down the stick" for God, he made a strong impact on his people.

Soon, other Masai began to be willing to consider the idea of "putting down the stick"—their way of saying "making a decision"—for Christianity.

Harold explained that spiritual rebirth is an individual thing, but that a group-oriented Masai will keep the decision secret or not make it at all if the older men say no.

"Masai don't listen passively and accept individually," Harold said. "They listen, discuss, let each person present an idea, and then come to a consensus."

So, the consensus to open up to missionaries takes awhile. About five years after Carl and Gerry opened work in Namanga, they ordained Paul Maseine as the first Baptist pastor among the Masai in Kenya.

But we weren't thinking about any of that as we stood around our disabled Cessna 210.

The Halls' homestead was out of reach and out of mind as Cordell, Jaston, Osten, and I gave a prayer of thanksgiving—surrounded by tall, lean Masai with red ochre caked in their hair and red cloth wrapped around their bodies.

Despite the work of missionaries and others, many Masai still haven't seen white people. Four-year-old Matamshi's father lifted him up so he could reach out to touch my skin while Cordell examined the engine and wiped off the oil which covered the plane.

Finally, Cordell decided to try to make it back to Nairobi, flying just above tree level down a road to provide a safe landing place if the engine caught fire.

Jaston Binala, an excitable young man with a lot of enthusiasm for life, punctuated our safe landing an hour later in Nairobi with a heartfelt, "Praise the Lord!"

That said it all in a part of the world where very little says it all, and one lives life constantly on the edge of discovery.

From day one in Africa, I've had to discover or rediscover a lot, including some things I'd always felt competent to do before.

Take something as "simple" as drying clothes.

When you have no dryer and live in a tropical climate you should be able to hang clothing outside to dry.

Right?

Wrong—at least not in Makwale.

Mango flies here lay eggs on anything, especially light-colored, fluttering garments hanging from a line. If those microscopic-size eggs aren't killed, they hatch out as tiny little things on your clothes.

Then they burrow into your skin, without you even feeling it, and begin to grow. About six weeks later you start to itch and then develop a pimple, which turns into a boil. When you squeeze the boil, a quarter-of-an-inch-long maggot pops out.

Try that the next time you want a "thrill!"

We solved the problem by hanging our clothes on a line in a long, screened-in porch we've built to link two buildings in our remodeled barn home. That way, we don't have to iron everything with our charcoal-heated iron.

Cooking, which I'd always excelled at in the United States, also called for relearning.

Most everything here is done from scratch without the prepared foods and shortcuts available to the American housewife.

For instance, if we want to have hamburger, we kill the cow first and grind the meat. Then we make our own buns, pickles, and catsup and hope we remembered to bring American-made mustard in the four-year supply of goods a missionary needs between furloughs in Tanzania. Otherwise, we make that, too.

Missionary wives must use a lot of ingenuity to put interesting, nourishing, American-type meals on the table for their families.

I compiled the first edition of *Out of Little . . . Much,* a cookbook with recipes from Tanzania missionary wives, which shows what they have learned to do in Tanzania. Kenya missionaries have done the same thing, but they have more prepared foods to use.

Our 242-page book has recipes to make such things as tea leaves, relish, soda crackers, pickles, catsup, vinegar, condensed milk, gelatin, marshmallows, noodles, malt, curry powder, meat tenderizer, tabasco sauce, mayonnaise, sourdough, mustard, crystallized fruit, and all sorts of things from scratch that you'd have to go back to the pioneer days of America to learn how to make.

It also has recipes for preparing dishes from appetizers to desserts, with little or no mixes or prepared foods, and it adds such extras as how to make finger paints for children and cockroach poison.

Occasional personal items pop up, such as the "Recipe for a Happy Missionary."

The ingredients for that are one cup each of consideration, courtesy, contentment, confidence, encouragement, helpfulness, interest in others, and blindness to their faults; two cups each of the milk of human kindness, praise, and carefully concealed flattery; one gallon of faith in God and others; one pinch of visitors; one generous dash of cooperation; one reasonable helpmate (optional); one trustworthy servant (optional); one large or several small hobbies, and three tablespoons of pure extract of "I am sorry."

Mix and "flavor with frequent portions of recreation and a dash of happy memories. Stir well and remove any specks of jealousy, temper, or criticism. Sweeten well with generous portions of love and keep warm with a steady flame of devotion. Never serve with a cold shoulder or hot tongue."

The book has served us well, but it can't completely make up for the shortages we face daily.

In the early days in Tukuyu, we could find meat at the African market. It's much more difficult now in these days of scarcity and economic deprivation.

Then, African shopkeepers killed a cow every morning, and we went to the market to buy the meat, standing in line with a handwoven shopping basket with the Africans.

The shopkeeper brushed away the flies and hacked off the chunk of our choice, and we went home to grind it and marinate it overnight, so it would be tender enough to chew.

Cooking is my temptation, and I have to be careful I don't spend too much time at it and overplan menus for the guests of all descriptions who pass through. Our area doesn't have restaurants or hotels, so hospitality is essential.

The real test comes during our crusades when my house helper, Paulo Kasunga, and I must tend, feed, and wash clothing for our volunteers from the United States who spread out all over the district, preaching three times a day in the dust and heat.

Take the 1984 crusade, for example. Paulo, a gentle little man with a huge capacity for work, helped me with field-marshal logistics—using our wood stove, charcoal iron, gasoline washing machine, and mango-fly-free porch clothesline.

We cared for ten volunteers and an assortment of ten others, including translators and support personnel. That called for fresh clothes every day for three weeks for twenty people, twenty vacuum bottles filled each morning and ready to take along to avoid parasites in the local water, breakfast on the table by 6:30 AM, an ice-cold glass of lemonade on standby when the team dragged in from a daily beating in a Land Rover, and dinner ready by 7:30 PM.

Paulo can cook pizza and make a lot of things himself, so we always planned something he knew how to cook on the days I went out with the volunteers.

We tried to prepare meals our visitors could enjoy after daily lunches of African cuisine strange to their stomachs such as African-style chicken and rice, beans, or fish with the head and eyes still intact, and, sometimes, even the national dish: *ugali.*

Africans place high emphasis on hospitality, and we warn our guests never to refuse to eat with them, even if the food seems strange. To do otherwise would be an extreme insult.

One visitor once summed it up like this: "Where you lead me, I will follow. What you feed me, I will swallow."

Tanzanians make *ugali* from ground corn just a little bit finer than grit meal. They boil it without salt, stirring it with a two-foot wooden spoon until it's so firm they can't stir anymore.

They shape it into a big mound, like a dome, and serve it with some type of greens—either bean leaves, squash leaves, or cabbage, cooked very soft and quite salty.

Africans gather around the common dish, roll up little balls of *ugali* in their fingers, and dip them into the thick, soft greens.

Another version of *ugali*—which tastes horrible to me—is sour *ugali,* made with soured corn and cooked without flavoring.

Africans may eat *ugali* once a day, usually after dark when they have their only cooked meal of the day. It's prepared by mothers who come in from the field, pound the corn in the backyard in a bowl made from a tree trunk, gather greens, collect firewood, and cook in a pot on three hard clay bricks on an open fire.

Plantains—cooking bananas—also boiled without seasoning, are even more common in the local diet, which may also include boiled white sweet potatoes, rice, beans, and casava.

A well-to-do family will have a breakfast consisting of tea with at least four spoons of sugar per cup. These days sugar is expensive and scarce, so not very many of them have tea anymore. They won't drink it without sugar.

If they get hungry during the day, they snack on guavas, mangos, bananas, or whatever fruit is in season.

Mothers may give children a little clump of *ugali* or a sweet potato to take to school for lunch.

Many Africans go for weeks, maybe months, without any complete protein. That leads to nutritional problems and illustrates the value of the well-rounded agricultural program Doug has emphasized.

Mostly, Africans feed foreign guests—such as our volunteers—chicken and rice.

They cook the rice to delicious perfection in a big clay pot with banana leaves over the top. It's much better than American rice, and I've rarely seen it burned, mushy, or gummy. But you have to take care not to break a tooth on a stray pebble which hasn't been sifted out.

Then, they kill a chicken, brown it a little, and boil

it in water, red palm oil, and a lot of salt until it's high in cholesterol but absolutely delicious.

It's quite a sacrifice for them to use one of their chickens, but they do it gladly to honor their guests. Edson enjoys rice and chicken more than any other dish. I can always count on him to say, "Mama, cook chicken and rice like the African women do."

Our two older children, Suzanne and Walter, came home to Tukuyu during breaks from Rift Valley Academy and have visited Makwale over the years. Walter came to Makwale for a year in 1981 to help Doug and me with the work.

But Richard and Edson, who are about nine years apart in age, spent the most time growing up in a strictly African environment—Richard in Tukuyu and Edson in Tukuyu and Makwale.

Edson is the most Africanized of the two. From birth, an African *ayah* (nurse) carried him around on her back, talking and singing to him. Ndymake, the young woman who caught cerebral malaria, was one. Geli, the wife of a man who helped Doug with agricultural work, was another.

Geli loved Edson very much and took care of him so I could teach Calvert correspondence lessons to Richard, one of the multiple duties of many missionary wives. She couldn't speak Swahili, like many other Africans Edson grew up with, but she talked to him constantly in Nyakyusa.

Edson was about a year-and-a-half old and just beginning to speak in sentences when my mother and father came to visit us in Tukuyu. His sentences weren't what Mother expected to hear.

"Ngalonda ulukama" ("I want some milk"), he said in Nyakyusa, running up to her.

She was shocked. The very idea of her grandchild growing up not speaking English! The fact she grew up speaking French didn't seemed to matter at that moment.

Not getting a satisfactory response, Edson tried again, changing beverages and languages.

"Nataka maji" ("I want some water"), he begged in Swahili, hoping Grandma would understand that.

She didn't.

Then he switched to English, which helped her a feelings little.

If she were alive now, Mother wouldn't worry. Edson has grown into an outstanding young man who can hold his own in Africa or America and speaks fluent English, Swahili, and Nyakyusa.

Most mothers take pride in their children's accomplishments. But missionary mothers, who often teach them through the elementary and junior-high-school years, have a special feeling when children succeed.

I'm proud of what all four of our children have accomplished in their education and in their lives. But the timing of our move to Africa allowed me to play a special role with Richard and Edson.

Some mothers find it difficult and frustrating to double as a schoolteacher, but it was a wonderful experience for me. I taught Richard second grade through the seventh and Edson first grade through the seventh in the Calvert program, except for furlough years and a brief time when missionary Sally

Conley taught Richard with her children while I
taught at the pastors training school in Tukuyu.

Richard went on to board at Rift Valley Academy
and excelled in all his education, from RVA through
the University of South Florida through medical
school.

Edson boarded at the International School of Mo-
shi, Tanzania, where he graduated with honors in the
international baccalaureate program before enroll-
ing in the University of South Florida to prepare for
seminary.

Both boys enjoyed their early years in Africa, running barefoot and playing in the dust with African
children.

We didn't like for them to go without shoes because of the worms they could pick up. But, as Richard remembers it, we finally gave up and let them do
it.

"Daddy doctored us and our dog—not necessarily
in that order—every four to six months with worm
pills, so we could enjoy ourselves," Richard said.

One thing Richard didn't enjoy was the weekly
dose of malaria suppressant we take because of the
malaria-bearing mosquitoes in the district. Many
Africans and missionaries call it either the "Sunday
medicine" or the "Sunday-Sunday medicine" because it's easy to remember to take it every Sunday.

I always told Richard to stick out his tongue and
put the bitter, white pills on the back, but it seldom
seemed to work for him. He gagged and said he got
headaches on Sunday mornings.

Richard also remembers that church was hard for
him as a child because he heard Doug preach the

same sermon over and over again until he finally learned Swahili well enough to come up with new ones.

But Richard made his profession of faith in an African church and was baptized by an African pastor, Anosisye Mwambaluma, whom he loved very much.

Richard claims he grew up on the run.

We had no refrigerator and no electricity for the first few months in Tukuyu. Finally, we got a kerosene refrigerator and a generator.

Richard earned part of his allowance by cutting the generator off each night. He tells it like this:

"A few minutes before nine o'clock, I'd put on my bathrobe and get my flashlight. I'd walk quickly through the wet grass, crouching low. It was real scary and dark out there.

"The generator would take thirty or forty seconds to wind down before all the lights went out. So I'd open the generator door, flip the switch, frantically lock the door, race back to the house at top speed, rush inside, and jump into bed.

"I got to where I could make it before the lights went off. My heart would pound as I dived under the covers. I've been running ever since."

Richard claims that conditioning saved him from the elephants when we had our close call in the jacked-up car.

It also made him famous in Tukuyu where he's still remembered as the *mzungu* who ran to church.

On Sundays, he'd run eleven miles from our house to church, usually accompanied about half the way by an African boy. I'd start out two hours later in a car and meet him.

Doug spent as much time with our boys as he could, taking them backpacking and mountain climbing whenever possible.

When Richard was a tenth grader, Doug accompanied him on an attempt on Mount Kilimanjaro.

They had only four days to make what should have been a five-day climb. Both made it to the hut at the twelve-thousand-foot level and barely made it the next day to the hut at the fifteen-thousand-foot level. Doug was so tired and weak from the altitude that night, he had to crawl to the rest room.

Scribbled on the wall next to the *choo* (toilet) were these words: "This is the dirtiest, highest, coldest john in all of Africa."

Those words may also rank as the poorest, highest graffiti in all of Africa.

It snowed that night, and when time came to rise at 2:00 AM for the assault on the peak, Richard went on alone, wearing only mid-topped suede shoes, while Doug waited and rested.

He made it to Gilman's Point at 18,600 feet but took the guides' advice not to try the remaining distance under existing conditions. Doug never tried it again, but both Richard and Edson have made it all the way to Uhuru Point, the highest spot in Africa at 19,340 feet.

Our years in Africa have had their high points and low points. A low one certainly came during our early months of trying to open work in Makwale, among people who feared we would shed blood in the valley.

8
Blood in the Valley

A pair of eyes peered out from behind an ancient baobab tree, watching every move Evelyn and I made.

That lone, gnarled, bulbous tree, which gave the illusion it grew upside down with roots pointing skyward, created a strange contrast to the rest of the scene.

Africans say God planted baobabs right side up, but *Shetani* (Satan) came during the night, uprooted them, and stuck them back in the ground upside down.

Baobabs are common to other areas of Tanzania but not to Kyela District. Somehow this single natural monstrosity had taken root there.

But the attitude of the man crouching behind it wasn't a rarity in those days as we began our work there.

"Hujambo, habari, Bwana?" ("Hello, how are things, Bwana"?), I called in greeting, starting toward him.

Suddenly, with the seeming speed of the graceful

gazelles which bound across the vast stretches of
Africa, he fled into a banana grove.

I dropped my outstretched hand, scuffed my toe in
the dirt, and shredded a banana leaf in frustration.

We were trying to get something started in Kyela,
but we couldn't seem to get to first base. Why did
they treat us like the plague? White faces were certainly strange to the Nyakyusa at that time, but a few
church people lived in the Makwale area and they
had accepted us.

However, pagans, who made up most of the population in that area, were skittish. They scattered like
leaves before the wind when we approached them in
a marketplace and scurried out the back when we
came to the front doors of their thatched, bamboo-
and-mud huts and called out, *"Hodi?"*

Instead of "May I come in?" *"Hodi?"* soon began
to mean, at least in our case, "Run, the *wazungu* are
coming!"

Finally, I gathered the African men we'd brought
down from Tukuyu to help start our demonstration
shamba (farm) and said, "Spread out among the people and find out what the problem is."

"They're afraid of you, Bwana Nepu," the men
told me when they returned.

"Afraid of me? Is a white face that strange around
here?"

"No, Bwana, it's not your white face. The *mchawi*
told them you have come to take their blood."

"The witch doctor told them what!?"

"That you've come to take their blood."

"Their blood?"

"Yes, the *mchawi* told them you want to use their blood to mix black magic potions in order to make yourself more powerful. He said if they get anywhere near you, you'll capture them and take their blood out."

Now that's a hard thing to overcome. I'd come to help them improve their agriculture and to tell them about Jesus, and they thought I wanted their blood.

As time progressed, Evelyn and I came face-to-face with the realities of pagan Africa, especially when a local Christian man's little boy succumbed to smallpox. When Baptists went to pay their respects and help with the funeral, they found the "native doctor" or witch doctor with many of the old pagan elders waiting to perform their rites.

That included cutting the stomach and intestines to determine if the child had been killed by a witch in his stomach or an evil spirit in his intestines. African Christians consider this an abominable practice, and the church strictly forbids it. But because the boy's old pagan grandfather insisted, the child's father gave in, and his Christian friends went away shaking their heads.

While Evelyn and I did all we could to break down fears about our motives for being there, we set out to clear the land for the farm, commuting down the mountain from Tukuyu as it developed.

The *shamba* got started after the Tanzanian government sent an expert to lay out a model village.

He came to this primitive area full of ideas he must have picked up in a course somewhere for urban planners. He had a "master plan" which blocked off areas for houses, a government center, a post office, churches, businesses, and the whole works.

When Makwale Baptist Church leaders would propose a location, he would said, "Oh, no. That's not zoned for a church. It's a residential area."

They'd never heard of "zoned" before, so the expert pulled out his "master plan" and tried, unsuccessfully, to explain it to them.

"Here," he finally said in frustration, pointing to an open area. "You can build the church here. If you develop it, we'll give you ten acres." Now, that's the kind of language they could understand, and they responded enthusiastically.

As I suspected then, the concept of "zoning" never caught on in that primitive bush country, and Makwale never turned out to be a model town. The "master plan" went the way of many innovations which have tried in vain to penetrate Africa.

But the ten acres turned into the Baptist *shamba*, which has grown to a hundred acres over the years and caused radical changes in crop production and animal husbandry in the Kyela District.

Meanwhile, Manasi, then the old pastor of the Makwale church, had some master plans of his own. He had visions of his small congregation occupying a mighty edifice.

Not satisfied with a mere thatched hut for a church, he had the members erect a false brick front. From a certain vantage point where he liked to stand, it made his church look like the latest thing in bush architecture. Not only Americans develop "edifice" complexes, it seems.

Inside, the old pastor built two pulpits of clay and manure molded around bamboo. He'd been impressed with the two-pulpit style of African Lutheran churches, one pulpit for reading Scripture and the other for preaching.

Manasi's vision shattered several weeks later when wind toppled the freestanding brick front and wrecked the church. The congregation, with typical African practicality, used the bricks for seats and surrounded them with the traditional thatched African building.

Today, the Makwale church is a large brick structure which will seat five-hundred people. In fact, about forty of the 250 Baptist churches in the Kyela District are all brick, but very few used bricks in the early days before explosive church growth began there.

Meanwhile, the new farm began to take shape as we carved a niche for it out of the completely undeveloped tropical forest, originally set aside as forest reserve by the British. When the country got independence, the government opened it up for settlement.

It took a lot of backbreaking labor to clear out the underbrush, cut trees, dig the stumps out by hand, fence the raw land, and begin construction of buildings—first a tool shed and then a barn. We converted the barn into our house when we moved there permanently a decade later.

Evelyn and I—and whatever combination of our children who were home from school—spent periods of days to weeks there as the farm developed. We lived first in a tent, then in the barn. We bathed in a stream, used an outdoor toilet, slept on handmade bamboo beds, and used a kerosene refrigerator and a camp stove we set up in one end of the barn. Eventually, we built a tin-roofed cook shed to keep the thatched roof from igniting.

Just like when we'd arrived in Tukuyu, I couldn't wait to plunge my hands into the soil at Makwale and see what I had to work with.

Tukuyu, at fifty-two-hundred feet altitude, has pumice soil formed from broken-down volcanic ash, unlike anything I'd ever seen. Makwale, at sixteen-hundred feet, a mile or so from the Livingstone Mountains, has fertile black soil, enriched by leaves and organic matter which filter down over the entire area from the steep mountains. It has temperatures which can range between one-hundred and one-hundred-twenty degrees, averaging in the eighties and nineties during the day and between sixty and seventy at night.

Our previous agricultural efforts at Tukuyu had made a real impression on government officials who came to visit and exclaim over our new crops or improved varieties.

Our biggest hit was improved coffee production. In those days, the government was more interested in export crops than food crops.

"Hunger will teach these people to plant corn, but our job is to encourage them to plant something that will bring income into the nation," a government agriculturist told me.

That's all changed now because Tanzania has faced

serious hunger problems like much of Africa. But many African governments still face the temptation to push cash crops because of their shaky economies.

Even then, Evelyn and I emphasized food production because we could see a lot of malnutrition and hunger, and I couldn't forget the silent message sent by the two little crosses at Makwale church. We began right away to experiment with a wide variety of things to change and enrich people's eating habits and thus improve their nutrition and health.

We ended up in some pretty strange situations in those early days in Tukuyu—such as the first night we visited a government leprosarium in old Rungwe District to hold an agricultural program.

The rain came down in torrents on the night the meeting was scheduled. Still, people flocked in, excited that *wazungu* had come. Soon 250 persons, most shielding themselves with hurriedly-cut banana leaves, had splashed barefooted through mud to the meeting.

They listened with interest as I read from the second chapter of Genesis:

> The Lord God planted a garden eastward in Eden; and there he put the man whom he had formed. And out of the ground made the Lord God to grow every tree that is pleasant to the sight, and good for food (Gen. 2:8-9).

Entranced, they listened as I explained how soil becomes tired and needs manure, how some foods help guard against diseases, and how others grow healthy bodies. They hung on every word because

their *shamba* is their life. An improved *shamba*
means an improved life.

"It's important to eat many kinds of food, not just
plantains and corn," I explained as they responded
enthusiastically to the packets of carrot, cabbage,
okra, turnip, onion, and bean seeds my family helped
me distribute.

But enthusiasm spilled over into near chaos when
I started to demonstrate a new "wonder" corn. With
great ceremony, I dropped a small handful of yellow
kernels into a big pot over a fire.

Suddenly, mysteriously, explosively—the pot filled
with white puffs—the likes of which they'd never
seen. But once they'd tasted it, they were convinced
and willing to try my advice on farming on their own
shambas. Popcorn never failed anywhere we held an
agricultural field day.

But the leprosarium group was different. Many of
the lepers gestured for us to pour the popcorn onto
their skirts or into a cloth because they had no hands
or were left with only stubs for fingers.

Just as He did when we looked into the eyes of the
derelicts in Kansas City, God pierced our hearts as
we looked beneath the diseased surface of the lepers
and saw human beings desperately in need of love.

Sadly, we realized many of them would never
leave the leprosarium because their bodies disinte-
grated as the disease grew worse. The improved
crops we offered were important to them but would
keep their bodies alive only for awhile. The love of
God would give them eternal spiritual life.

They realized that, too. "Will you come back and

help us start a Baptist church?" they pleaded as we prepared to leave. The church which resulted is one of many which has started because of agricultural missions in places where people from all walks of life have gathered to hear about agriculture and stayed to hear the gospel preached.

Now, the situation for lepers there is better. Much-improved treatment has greatly reduced the number of patients in the colony. Most lepers come to clinics in their local areas and receive medicine from the government. Many recover after a few years' treatment.

As I visited from *shamba* to *shamba* in those early days, I learned many lessons more valuable than the ones I taught. One was about the importance of never missing an opportunity to invite people to accept Jesus Christ.

One day, nearly two-hundred persons turned out for an agricultural field day at a small church on Lake Nyasa where the pastor was a fisherman.

At the close, I gave a short evangelistic message and urged the people to return to church, so they could learn more. Then I began the closing prayer.

I'd decided not to extend an invitation to accept Christ as Savior because most of the audience was made up of pagans. I thought it was too much to expect them to accept Christ after hearing the very first presentation of the plan of salvation.

Suddenly, a man stood up in the middle of the prayer and cried out, "I want to accept Christ now!"

That man and another in the crowd came forward and made their professions of faith. Members of the small, struggling church were ecstatic over even two new converts and became encouraged to renew their efforts to reach others. Since that day, I've always issued an invitation at agricultural meetings, funerals, or anywhere else I speak. Many Africans have accepted Christ as a result.

What a change to move from a responsive area like that to a place like Makwale where Africans ran at the sight of me, convinced I'd come for their blood.

While we looked for a way to dispel that fear, I consoled myself with developing the land, and what a beautiful land it was. It had impressed me from the first and captivated me completely when we left language school and drove some six-hundred miles, mostly over unpaved road, from Dar es Salaam to Tukuyu in late 1964 to begin our work in Tanzania's Southern Highlands.

The Knapp family must have made quite a spectacle jammed into our Volkswagon beetle with Richard, a German Shepherd, two rabbits, and assorted odds and ends. Thankfully, we had sent our household goods in a truck.

We left at 4:00 AM and drove straight through, pushing hard to make it in one day. Veteran Africa hands would have had better sense than that. They would have stretched such a long, rough journey to at least two days.

But we were eager rookies. Besides that, we were a little skittish. We didn't want to stop anywhere because of anti-American demonstrations taking place at various points around the country at that time.

We covered the deeply rutted, five-hundred-mile "Hell's Run" from Dar es Salaam without incident. Columns of dust left by a truck could be seen for ten miles along that tortuous, aptly-named road. It wouldn't be paved until the early 1970s.

As we reached the turnoff to Tukuyu near Mbeya, anticipation grew, and so did the impact of this beautiful country of contrasts which changed terrain and vegetation as the miles passed by. It was like moving from one world into another and then another.

We approached the Mporoto Mountains, coiffed with the mist which rises to the top of the mountains from Lake Nyasa in the moist Kyela valley to the south. The parched air on the Mbeya side holds the mist at bay.

Sammy DeBord and those after him had penetrated beyond that mist for Southern Baptist missions, but the adventure excited us nonetheless as we finally neared the beginning of our long-awaited mission career.

We passed small, irregular fields of wheat which gave way to stretches of pyrethrum, potatoes, cabbage, and English peas as we gained altitude. As we climbed, each mile brought a heavier rainfall area with consequent changes in vegetation.

We passed bamboo forests, interspersed with giant, red-ribbed leaves of wild banana trees, and entered the home country of the Safwa Tribe.

Off to the right, a roving "circumcision band" of thirty African boys and girls, with faces painted white, danced about and serenaded us to the accom-

paniment of bells and drums. They had reached the
age of twelve, the time for circumcision and then
adulthood, and they celebrated that fact with traditional ceremony as we gawked at the newness of it
all.

At eighty-five-hundred feet, we began a slow de-
scent, the rutted road winding through beautiful al-
pine forests, which soon gave way to agricultural
development and denser population. In 1967, German road builders would pave the road with Tarmac,
but then it was rutted and treacherous.

Plots of coffee, along with corn and vegetables,
greeted us as we reached lower climes. So did an
increasing number of little white crosses, inscribed
with the words, *"Kanisa la Kibatisti"* (Baptist
Church). Then we passed the "mother church" of the
area, Jerusalem Baptist Church, founded in 1958 by
Sammy DeBord and Anosisye Mwangwembe, after
Anosisye finally prevailed on Sammy to cross the
mountain.

As we passed the village of Kiwira, we entered the
heartland of the mountain Nyakyusa people. Every
inch of the area, it seemed, was cultivated in two-to-
five-acre family *shambas*.

We slowed to a crawl, picking our way with trepi-
dation through a road full of people enroute to the
market with produce. Even in normal daily living,
driving is hazardous in Africa where most people
walk oblivious to cars. Under these conditions, honk-
ing can be a lifesaver rather than a discourtesy, especially when two cars travel close together.

Africans may step aside for one car, but after it

passes they will likely stray back onto the road into the path of the other, not dreaming there could be a second car way out in the bush country.

Women, colorful cloth *kangas* wrapped about their bodies and their heads, swayed under their burdens—babies in cloth slings on their backs and large baskets of produce on their heads. African women have it rough, especially in the bush where life usually involves second-class status in the male-dominated society, endless work, and childbearing. Life expectancy is low and, as in most of Africa, age is venerated.

The scene, still strange to our eyes, was dominated to the east by Mount Rungwe, a ten-thousand-foot extinct volcano, and later along the way by Mount Kyejo, its smaller sister volcano. Mount Kyejo is still considered active.

Passing Rungwe Tea Estate, with its endless fields of manicured tea plants, we entered Tukuyu, a town of about fifteen hundred. It was the central and only town then in old Rungwe District.

We collapsed that night in the home of Bill and Nina Lewis and then geared up the next day for the chore of moving into an attractive brick house the Baptist Mission had acquired for us.

Situated on the edge of a magnificent cedar forest about a mile above sea level, it had a spectacular view of the Livingstone Mountains and the entire valley leading down to Lake Nyasa. Southward toward the lake, the altitude drops off rapidly and the land levels off into a steaming plain.

With no electricity available, we would have no

refrigeration until we got a kerosene refrigerator. That took six months. We used to think we couldn't go a week without refrigeration.

Unpacking the crates, which arrived the next day, went quickly until I came across the one holding the seeds I'd carefully packed in Florida. Suddenly, the need to get down to the task we'd come for overwhelmed me.

The place was a mess, unpacked boxes and items of furniture everywhere. That could wait—in my opinion, though not in Evelyn's. She thought the garden should wait until we had finished unpacking. But the lure of the soil temporarily overcame her disapproval. As I plunged my hands into the loosened earth and began to plant the seeds, I could feel the tension ease. At last, after all these months on hold, I was getting down to work.

Now, as we began anew at Makwale, the same sense of relief and accomplishment enveloped me as the demonstration farm began to take shape. It gave me something constructive to do while I dealt with the frustration of not even being able to talk to many local people without them running in fear.

Missionaries spend long periods on hold from their work as they prepare for the mission field, go through language school, get their families established, spend time on furlough, and accomplish everything else that goes into the logistics of missions living. It calls for patience and perseverance, especially in an environment like Africa where no one seems to hurry.

Most Africans insist on doing everything slowly

and with dignity by what even some of them call "African time." Events start when everyone gets there and end when everyone's ready to leave. Church services, for example, can go on for hours. What doesn't get done tomorrow can get done the next day, the next, or the next . . .

Africans don't let time rush them, but they don't ignore it. Unless an overcast day diminishes their accuracy, Africans, especially those who live outside larger towns, can estimate time to within an hour, a half, or even a quarter hour, by noting the position of the sun. In Swahili, time is measured from daybreak to sunset, as it was in biblical days.

In one sense, African time adds to the quality of life. But it certainly frustrates time-conscious, result-oriented Westerners.

Time wore on as the farm developed at Makwale, our fruit and vegetables began to grow abundantly, and our *ng'ombe* (cows) and *kuku* (chickens) produced large amounts of *maziwa* (milk) and *mayai* (eggs).

Even from a distance, the Nyakyusa could tell the difference.

The *mahindi* (corn) grown in that area was unimproved from its introduction into Africa hundreds of years ago. It took nine months for them to produce a low-quality crop with small ears little better than Indians were growing when early settlers arrived in Colonial America.

The Nyakyusa could see our fast-growing corn prospering across the fence with great big ears, and their eyes got bigger the more they looked.

They could also see our cows with great big bags of milk. Their little cows gave just a pint per milking.

Our big chickens and big eggs also made an impression.

One thing is universal. When farmers see something they think will help their farms, they've got to have it. Eventually, they began to sidle up to the fence, keeping well out of reach, and ask in Swahili:

"What kind of *mahindi* is that which has such big ears, with such fine kernels, and grows so fast?"

Or:

"What kind of *ng'ombe* is that which has such a big bag of *maziwa* to drink?"

Or:

"What kind of *kuku* is that which lays such big *mayai?*"

Soon, we started sending out seeds and hatching eggs for them to try. They wouldn't come and get them, but our gifts—a true sign of friendship and hospitality in that culture—began to break the ice.

Before too many months, they began to get bolder because so far we had done nothing but good for them—and hadn't even once tried to draw anyone's blood.

One afternoon, I noticed a man watching as I worked near a storage shed. He seemed to want to speak, but he didn't know how to begin.

"Hujambo, habari, Bwana," I called out in greeting.

"Sijambo," he answered tentatively.

He shuffled nervously and mumbled something almost unintelligible, but I caught the word *mbegu.*

He wanted *mbegu*—seeds. But he was afraid to come get them.

Gesturing for him to wait, I went inside the shed and emerged with a packet of corn seeds. Already, local farmers were beginning to get good results with them.

I talked to him pleasantly of the beautiful day and how happy I was to give him seeds for his family as I slowly drew nearer.

Suddenly alert, his body tensed as if to spring.

"Have you noticed how these *mbegu* grow big ears of *mahindi?*" I asked, stopping out of reach.

"Ndio," he responded in the affirmative.

I wanted to rush up, take him by the hand, and tell him I'd come to be his friend, but African patience had begun to teach me a lesson. Laying the packet of corn seeds carefully on the ground, I backed away.

"Take this," I said. "I'll be glad to help you if you have any problems planting them. There are some special things you can do to make the soil better for crops."

Taking another step back, I added, "Come back tomorrow, and I will give you *mbegu* for that." I pointed toward some fruit trees which had begun to make a hit with the Africans.

By this time the farm consisted of a few acres of cleared land, planted in trial plots of corn, soybeans, and other vegetables. Fruit trees, raised from seedlings brought in a suitcase from Florida or collected from botanical gardens in Kenya and Tanzania, lined the stream which angled across the farm. Young coconut trees brought from Dar es Salaam were beginning to take root.

Cocking his head to keep a careful eye on me, he bent over, scooped up the packet, and darted away.

Suddenly, he realized he had violated African politeness and failed to say thank you.

"*Asante sana, Bwana,*" he called with a wave as he disappeared into the brush.

"Thank you very much also, Bwana," I responded under my breath, "for coming near enough to talk."

The next day, I kept an eye peeled for him as I worked, but he didn't show up. Another failure: Would I have patience to stay here under these conditions?

But two days after that he was back—true to "African time."

We went through the same routine over the days to come until, finally, he had a sample of everything I had. Then one day, I noticed him standing and watching.

"You have some of all the seeds I have right now," I said. "I have nothing to offer you today but a cup of *chai.* Would you do me the honor of coming to my home for some *chai?*"

Refusal of an offer of tea would be an extreme breach of African hospitality.

Noticeably perplexed, he took a step nearer.

"I do not understand you, Bwana," he said. "The *mchawi* said you had come to steal our blood to make bad *dawa* (medicine). But you have done nothing but give us good things. Why do you do this?"

"Have you noticed how the *mbegu* you plant in the ground make an abundant harvest?" I asked.

"*Ndio.*"

"I have come with a message from *Kyala,* the one true God, about what you can plant in your life so you can have an abundant harvest of good things there also. Do you want me to tell you how to do that?"

"*Ndio.*"

"As you noticed, I do not want to take your blood. But Jesus Christ, *Kyala's* only Son, gave His own blood so that you can come to know *Kyala* and have the good things He wants you to have."

He listened attentively as I explained how he could find forgiveness for his sins and eternal life. As shadows cast by the setting sun grew long in the Kyela valley, he knelt to pray for Jesus to come into his life.

"When was it that *Kyala* sent Jesus to save us?" he asked when he arose.

"It was a long time ago, almost two-thousand years."

"Why did it take so long for you to come and tell me about it?" he asked in amazement, adding before I could answer: "If only I had heard about this when I was a boy. It would have made a great difference in my life."

A breakthrough had begun in our work in the valley—not with a crash of thunder this time but with the still, small voice of God penetrating a human heart.

9
Jitihada

Blue-green waves of the Indian Ocean, warmed by the sun, soothed the pain radiating through my hands, arms, neck, and head.

I'll have to try this therapy for "Land Rover neck" more often, I thought.

"Land Rover neck"—that's another of the hazzards of Africa they hadn't told us about in the beginning. It's a condition of the neck and upper spine developed over many years of crushing jolts on rough bush roads where your spine expands and compresses like a bellows or a shock absorber as the heavy-duty Land Rover rises and falls.

In my own case, one neck disc has collapsed and arthritis has set in, partially closing the nerve passages which reach my arms, neck, and head. Use of the arms to drive long distances, carry anything heavy, or baptize large numbers of people causes numbness and pain. A neck brace helps.

"Land Rover neck" was the only thing which could come anywhere near spoiling that wonderful day of relaxation after five weeks of intensive work from morning until night in distant Makwale.

Green-and-gold coconut palms, gracefully bending along the windswept shoreline, waved to me as I lolled in the surf in front of the Bahari Beach Hotel, near Dar es Salaam and a few miles from where missionary Wimpy Harper had drowned twenty-seven years earlier.

Sounds of waves crashing onto the white sand and sails crackling as Arab *dhows* tacked into the wind sent me no message.

Not so with the guttural refrain of the frogs in Makwale. Frogs croak endlessly as the twilight deepens at the foot of the Livingstones. Lately, their song had seemed to say in Swahili:

"*Jitihada. Jitihada. Jitihada.*"

"Crusade. Crusade. Crusade."

A crusade indeed. Five weeks of crusade with two teams of twenty-two volunteer laypersons and preachers from the United States and five Tanzanian preachers had produced 13,823 decisions for Jesus Christ. That included 12,657 first-time professions of faith, our largest total yet in Kyela District.

More than ten-thousand people in the home churches of the volunteers had supported the effort with around-the-clock prayer chains.

My attention strayed to the beach where sunbathers, mainly white European tourists, worked on their skin cancer. I wondered if they could conceive of life in the distant bush country from which I'd just come.

Africans certainly couldn't conceive of their lifestyle. A group of African workers, there to build a new, circular hotel dining room from hand-chiseled stone, stood along a balcony gawking in disbelief at the tourists' scanty attire.

Clad in hard hats and ragged clothing, these men worked hard to avoid the nakedness of their bush-dwelling ancestors. They equated clothing with civilization and just could not understand why these *wazungu,* who had everything they envied, would run around nearly naked.

Life is full of such paradoxes. Take our quest for a soft drink, for example.

At the very moment when many people in America were feuding over whether "New Coke" would replace old Coke or whether they could have a choice of the two, Evelyn and I, fresh from our draining crusade, would have settled for any kind of Coke.

We thought maybe we could find some for us and a visitor from the United States at the hotel restaurant. It had been a long time between Cokes.

"Please bring us three Coca-Colas with ice, Bwana," I said in English to the waiter, phrasing each word carefully for his Swahili-tuned ear.

Oh, boy, I thought. *Will that taste good!*

"We do not have any, Bwana," he replied in his precise Afro-British English.

Our stilted exchange continued.

"Oh, that is too bad. Please give us three Fantas" (bottled fruit drinks).

We drank our Fantas with much less gusto than we would a Coke.

Then we began to notice that other customers were getting Cokes.

"Bwana, those people have Cokes," I exclaimed shifting into Swahili. "You said you didn't have any."

The little man responded nervously in Swahili.

"It's true, Bwana, but they bought spirits to go with their Cokes."

The picture became clear. We couldn't have any of the hotel's scarce Cokes unless we ordered liquor to go with them. That's one way to deal with shortages and make some extra money besides.

"Baptists don't drink spirits," I told the waiter in my most emphatic Swahili. "Please let us have some Coca-Cola."

The answer was still no.

But we had our taste buds set for a cold Coke. Finally, I said, "Bwana, let me pay you for both the Coca-Colas and the spirits. But you bring us only the Coca-Colas. OK?"

"Oh, no, Bwana, that would be an economic crime."

Oh! I thought. *It's OK to make me buy liquor with my Coke, but it's not OK for me to pay for something I don't get, even if I don't want it.*

But that was that, and we thought the discussion had ended.

The next day, I said, "Bwana, please bring us three Fantas."

"I am sorry, Bwana, we do not have any Fantas, but we have some Coca-Colas."

"But, I thought . . ." I stopped short. Why fight it? We'd learned long ago that if you don't like something in Africa just wait awhile and it will change, often for no apparent reason.

We took the Cokes without batting an eye, and thoroughly enjoyed them—not caring whether they were old, new, or middle-aged.

And, best of all, we'd gotten them with no suspicion of "economic crime," a much-used phrase in Tanzania these days. The government has cracked down on all types of economic corruption which can possibly contribute to black markets and price hiking.

You can't be too careful in avoiding overzealous enforcement. In fact, Walden Kamomonga, one of our Baptist pastors in Kyela District, once spent six months in jail before he could prove his innocence of economic crimes.

During a crackdown to stop black marketeering, police found seventy-two bags of unhulled rice Walden had grown on his *shamba* and bicycle parts and other items worth more than $8,330, which he had left over from a legitimate shop he had closed several months before.

The court finally freed him for lack of evidence and allowed him to return to his wife and six children. Meanwhile, he had won six of his fellow prisoners to Jesus Christ.

That kind of spirit of winning people wherever you find them lies at the heart of the evangelistic breakthroughs of recent years in the Kyela District. As we've said, each person counts, and the bucket fills— drop by drop.

I've gotten out of touch with sports after more than two decades in Africa, but I understand that's the way Pete Rose of the Cincinnati Reds broke Ty

Cobb's supposedly unbreakable major-league baseball record for career base hits.

Ironically, Rose did it one hit at a time—drop by drop—between 1963 and 1985, beginning the same year we were appointed as missionaries to Tanzania.

In fact, some of our volunteer laypersons and preachers kept tabs on him during our most recent crusade. Short-wave radio brought reports all the way out to Makwale on Rose's record-breaking exploits at the same time we were on the way to the 12,657 conversions, which may be a record for an association of churches on any Southern Baptist foreign mission field.

On September 8, 1985, while American media brimmed with news of Rose tying Cobb at 4,191 hits, news was spreading in Kyela District by word of mouth that *Jitihada* had topped eleven-thousand conversions, some thirty-five hundred higher than our previous associational record. Jaston Binala, a schoolteacher and writer in Tanzania, reported the final total about a week later in *Sauti Ya Wabatisti*, a newsletter of the Kyela Baptist Association.

Short-wave radio reported that Rose broke Cobb's record on September 11 and ended the 1985 season with 4,204 hits. But our "season" in Kyela District goes on, 365 days a year, as we seek to continue to win new converts, baptize them, and provide follow up training.

The series of crusades got started in the district in the first place, not because we had a brainstorm, but because the Baptist Mission of Tanzania decided that

each station should have an evangelistic crusade in
1976. They assigned us four American volunteers.

The 1976 crusade resulted in four-hundred professions of faith, the largest total in the country that
year. That made us realize we hadn't spent enough
time over the years reaping a harvest from spiritual
seeds we'd been sowing. So we decided to hold a
crusade about every other year after that.

Each crusade has something memorable. Several
things come to mind about the 1985 effort, featuring
American volunteers from several Florida Baptist
churches.

Memories stand out sharply of Leo Bushanga, age
nine, and of Mellie Smith, a laywoman from First
Baptist Church of Lake Wales, Florida.

I'll never forget Leo, whom I ran over with a truck,
or Mellie, who has gifts of storytelling perfectly
matched to African culture.

First, let me tell you about Mellie. She averaged
more than 112 professions of faith per outing. That's
more than any of her male counterparts, layman or
pastor, who did very well in their own right. The two
teams consisted of fourteen laypersons, five pastors,
and three church staffers.

Mellie's husband sold his boat so she could afford
to come, and she made the best of it.

Leo got the best of it, too. He survived, after much
prayer on our part, with no permanent injuries.

He and several other typically irrepressible African children clambered into the back of my pickup
truck as I left a school where we'd held an evangelistic service.

Leo missed his footing, fell under the pickup, and was run over by a rear wheel which left tire marks across his body and a large cut on his head.

I prayed fervently as I frantically drove him to the nearest hospital, about an hour away.

On the way, I met one of the volunteers, David Holder, a physician from Winter Park, Florida, and was never happier to see anyone.

David examined him and accompanied me to the hospital where Leo was admitted for treatment.

I reported the accident to the police. They allowed me to continue working in the crusade but asked me to surrender my vehicle and driver's license.

That created real problems for our schedule. Team members had to double up and do more driving than we planned as we fanned out over the Kyela District for crusade sessions in churches and schools.

Joy and relief overwhelmed us several days later when word came that God had answered our prayers and healed Leo completely.

After his release from the hospital, the police returned my car and license and made no charges because Leo had recovered and because I hadn't known the children were on the truck.

More importantly, the news of God's healing power added impact to the crusade services which had started slowly with only twenty-eight professions of faith on the first day and fifty-nine on the second day. Team members later reported 1,487 in a single day.

Gary Folds, pastor of Second Baptist Church, Ma-con, Georgia, had a similar experience with God's healing power during our 1982 crusade.

A crowd of people blocked the road as Gary attempted to drive to a crusade preaching point. Gary was afraid to stop, but his interpreter recognized some people in the crowd.

"Don't be afraid to stop," he said. "Some of these are Christian people. Let's stop and see what they want."

"We have two sick people in our village," a spokesman explained. "Please come and treat them."

"I'm sorry, I'm not a doctor," Gary responded. "I can't help you. I don't have any medicine."

They wouldn't take no for an answer.

"Please come help," they insisted. "These people are very sick, and they will die if you don't help us."

"Well, I will come and pray for them," Gary said.

He followed his interpreter and a guide from the village down a side path until they came to a little thatched hut.

A man lay inside, showing no signs of life. Relatives, expecting him to die, were already gathering for a funeral.

Gary fell down on his knees and prayed for the man, and then the interpreter prayed. They also prayed at another hut where a man, apparently with a severe case of pneumonia, was barely able to breathe.

Then Gary and the interpreter hurried back to the car and drove to the outdoor preaching site.

A loud commotion interrupted the service several minutes after Gary began preaching. A large number of people joined the crowd. Looking out over the crowd, Gary suddenly thought he recognized the men he had prayed for. Almost too stunned for words, he stopped the service and asked through the interpreter:

"Are you the men I just prayed for?"

"Yes," two voices responded. "God has healed us."

Amazement rippled through the crowd because it was widely known the men were ill and expected to die.

Gary told other crusade volunteers about the experience that night, and they began praying for the sick as they encountered them. Other healings occurred, but only one rivaled the first two. That involved a brother of a translator, who recovered from meningitis after prayer at a hospital.

As word spread, large numbers of people started attending the services. The healings created enormous interest among the pagans who are attuned to the supernatural and respond to concrete, physical demonstrations of God's power.

In a society where people accept the reality of the supernatural, we've found God will often manifest startling New-Testament displays of miraculous power to establish Himself as superior to false deities.

That happens less in societies where people's so-called sophistication shuts them off from faith in supernatural solutions.

Other missionaries have observed the same thing. For example, Dwight and Lila Reagen, who work among the Indian population in Durban, South Africa, have found that Hindus will listen to suggestions to call on Jesus Christ in time of crisis, after witchcraft and their myriad gods have failed, because they're attuned to calling on spiritual powers.

Often, the result has been a miraculous healing or life-changing event which has so impressed Hindus with the power of God that they've either accepted Christ as Savior or become open to the possibility.

An Indian Baptist schoolteacher in Durban once reported she prayed for a mute girl in her classroom and then asked her a question.

The child answered and after that talked normally.

"Ma'am, you have magic in you!" shouted the startled pupils.

"It's not magic," she said, "but the power of God."

God's power and prayer certainly influenced results of our six crusades in Kyela District between 1976 and 1985. After the 400 professions of faith in 1976, we recorded totals of 800; 1,300; 7,505; 4,119; and 12,657 in succeeding crusades.

The 1982 crusade, our second largest, provides several strong examples of the power of prayer.

Many Tanzanians and about fourteen-hundred people in American churches joined in an around-the-clock prayer chain during that crusade. It needed all that and more, just to get started.

We planned for the ten American volunteers, each covering four to six areas a week over a three-week period, to concentrate on the newer, smaller churches in the district.

Our analysis from the 1980 crusade, led by volunteers from Arkansas, revealed that most decisions came from services in villages where churches had just started with about a dozen members.

In many such situations, hundreds had made decisions in response to the enthusiastic efforts of new converts, while only a comparative few made decisions in the older, more established areas.

We also planned to get into the public schools where we were allowed to preach.

As the time for the crusade approached, we began having problems. I arrived at the airport in Dar es Salaam at 2:00 AM to pick up members of the team and learned one of them hadn't been able to come. We had no replacement preacher for him or for another of the team who was sick with what we call "tourist disease"—nausea, vomiting, and diarrhea.

We had to leave early the next morning so Missionary Aviation Fellowship's small plane could make two trips to get the team to Mbeya before dark. The airport there has no landing lights.

The sick man, James Tisdale, a pastor from Alabama, was in no condition to fly, so we delayed him until the second group. But the first group almost didn't take off.

"I'm sorry, but I left the switch on last night in the plane," the embarrassed MAF pilot said. "My battery's dead, and I can't get the engine started."

Since he had no way right then to get the battery charged, the pilot tried to start it by spinning the prop, but he wore himself out and nothing happened.

We knelt and prayed right there on the runway.

Someone got up and left us as we prayed, but we continued without looking up.

When we finished, our pilot was walking back holding a battery.

"I felt led to open my eyes while we were praying," he said, "and I saw a friend getting ready to take off. He agreed to let us use his battery to start my engine. I'll start it and switch to my battery. By the time we get to Mbeya, my battery will be charged up enough to restart the engine for the return trip."

That group arrived safely, but time was running out as we prepared to send the second group. We delayed as long as possible because a key Nyakyusa-speaking translator, Simon Mwakalinga, hadn't shown up, and James Tisdale was still too sick to fly.

Again, prayer made the difference.

James's illness disappeared almost immediately after we knelt and prayed. Then we prayed for Simon's arrival but finally had to leave for the airport without him so we could make it to Mbeya by dark. But Simon made it, performing the unlikely feat of finding us in the hectic Dar es Salaam traffic.

After all that, the healing episodes experienced by Gary Folds shouldn't have surprised us—or all the other things that happened.

Bill Robinson, a layman from Grapevine, Texas, was scheduled to preach at a church, but his translator got sick, and no one at the church could translate from English to Nyakyusa.

A chance visitor from Malawi, there to visit relatives, stopped by to practice his English when he saw Bill and agreed to stay and translate.

When Bill extended the invitation, the translator turned toward him as others responded and said, "I, too, want to accept that invitation to believe in Jesus Christ."

At another service, Bobby Welch, pastor of First Baptist Church, Daytona Beach, Florida, had a translator but almost didn't get to use him. Bobby, who assembled the crusade team for us, preached at a school where the young people were studying English and refused translation. They were determined to hear it in English.

Before the service began, Bobby recalled that a group of men in his church in Daytona Beach were meeting at that exact time to pray for him. As the service progressed, Bobby realized the young people weren't really following what he had to say, but he continued. When he gave an invitation to accept Jesus Christ, no one responded.

"Can't we go over that again with a translator?" Bobby asked.

The young people, proud of their English, shouted down the idea.

Finally, the principal intervened. "A lot of them didn't understand," he said. "We'll have it translated."

Bobby preached again, this time through translator Osten Mwakijungu, and two-hundred young people accepted Christ—the exact number in the men's prayer group meeting at that moment in Florida.

One of the volunteers, a teenager named Ben Halliday, had come along to help out, not to preach. We asked him to fill in for the missing team member. He hesitated, but his pastor said, "Don't worry, we'll give you a sermon every night, and you can study it, preach, and do the best you can."

Ben went out with our prayers. The first day he preached at a church so remote visitors can reach it only in the dry season by driving across rice paddies. Thirty-two people accepted Christ.

He came back so excited he couldn't wait to go at it again. He ended up recording three hundred professions of faith. Ben, who later returned to Tanzania for awhile to help us with church-building projects, said the preaching experience later led to a call by God for him to become a preacher.

The 1982 crusade exceeded our wildest dreams. We had set a goal of 2,000 professions of faith, certainly reasonable after 1,300 in 1980. We topped that on the third day and kept going until we reached 7,505.

Jubilation reigned in our churches. The astounding results revolutionized many of our little dozen-member churches, which suddenly had fifty to a hundred new believers from their own villages. Church membership in the district jumped from 7,880 in 1982 to 14,245 in 1983.

For the first time, our people really began to realize that God could do something big in the Kyela District. He can do big things all over Tanzania and has done so in the work of many of our missionary colleagues.

Some twenty-one volunteer evangelistic teams led

crusades throughout Tanzania in 1984-85 in an effort which dovetailed with an East-Africa-wide emphasis by missionaries on Sunday School development.

Such efforts led to good statistical increases throughout the country. Baptisms increased from 8,718 in 1984 to 12,562 in 1985; membership from 44,527 to 50,960; Sunday School enrollment from 10,794 to 16,821; churches and preaching points from 737 to 788; and Woman's Missionary Union enrollment from 5,412 to 6,332.

Crusade results, which came in slowly from the remote areas, tell a powerful story. For example, 3,498 persons accepted Christ during a two-week crusade in the new Rungwe District, led by volunteers from Virginia, Georgia, Texas, and California, and effectively planned by missionary Olan Burrow.

Converts included many schoolteachers, village leaders, and even some village chiefs—former rulers under the old tribal system who still have great prestige.

Tanzanian Baptists met a week after that for their annual convention meeting and a national evangelism conference. They pledged to unite efforts to start new Sunday Schools throughout Tanzania, renew efforts to win people to Christ, and train teachers to win people *"bega kwa bega"* ("shoulder to shoulder") with the pastors.

Earlier, missionaries David and Betty Ann Whitson involved volunteers from Texas and North Carolina and African pastors and choirs in a four-day crusade in Bukoba.

David and Betty Ann love the Tanzanian people.

In 1983, they spearheaded a drive to inoculate fif-
teen-thousand children in their region against
measles, which accounts for 30 percent of all hospital
deaths in Tanzania.

The Whitsons began the effort when one of the
Baptist pastors attended a conference and reported
all four of his children had died from measles. His
wife had blamed him for the deaths and left him. He
felt his life was ruined. They spent most of the conference talking about what could be done to protect
other children.

Their crusade in Bukoba reported nearly a thousand decisions for Christ and some heartwarming
results in the lives of people. It made some Africans
forget their personal problems, a significant achieve-
ment in a country where people have so many needs.

"My choir and I will never be the same," African
pastor Lewis Joseph told Betty Ann after the crusade.

He related this story:

"We were at a most difficult place, where water
and food were scarce, and all of us were rather dis-
turbed by the lack of physical comfort. Yet each
morning, a crippled woman named Maliadena, who
could only crawl, brought us warm water for washing, served us river-water tea, and cooked for our
group of nine.

"In the evening, she'd bring us water for washing
again and prepare a hot meal of bananas and beans.
She was always so cheerful, so thrilled with recount-
ing how the services had blessed her, and so happy
that many were responding to the gospel.

"Maliadena has crawled for twenty of her twenty-six years. She has insufficient clothing and harsh, unsympathetic parents. But daily she requested prayer for her family and overflowed with joy when her mother accepted Christ during the crusade.

"As we left, my young people began to talk about how they could help her. This was such a change, for they're poor by many standards and usually just think of themselves.

"It opened my eyes. I must teach my people more about ministering to others."

Cripples like Maliadena are commonplace in Tanzania. Polio and other debilitating diseases leave many with twisted limbs in Third World countries where treatment is hard to get.

After the 1982 crusade, Bill Billingsley, pastor of Sheridan Hills Baptist Church in Hollywood, Florida, determined to do something about the cripples he had seen in Kyela District Baptist churches.

Sheridan Hills sent us ten hand-propelled, triwheel vehicles to give to needy church members.

We'll never forget the day thirty-one-year-old Gwamaka Mwakifuge, crippled since childhood by polio, "exchanged" his withered legs for wheels at a presentation before his entire village.

Villagers began to clap and warble the high-pitched *vigelegele* as Gwamaka experimented and then finally mastered the combination bicycle and wheelchair. His affliction had limited his travel to only a few hundred yards from his home, walking on hand blocks, and dragging his legs behind him. Now he could travel over a twenty-mile area without assistance.

Gwamaka drove joyously in wide sweeping circles and then stopped in front of us.

"Jesus really does care," he said, breaking into a broad grin.

Another cripple gave Gary Folds an unforgettable illustration of what dedication is all about.

We were driving rapidly down a banana-tree-lined trail, late for a preaching engagement in a bush church during the 1982 crusade. Suddenly, we saw a man up ahead crawling on his hands and knees, and I braked quickly, thinking at first he was injured. Polio had twisted his legs, and he had terrible callouses on his hands and knees.

"Where are you going that you'd be willing to crawl to get there?" I asked.

"I'm a Baptist, and my church is back there," he said, gesturing into the trees. "It's too little for the American preacher to come there, so I'm going to another church to hear him. But I can't move fast. I'm afraid I'll be late."

"Don't worry, you're not going to be late," I said. "I have Bwana Folds, the preacher, right here."

We picked him up, put him in the car, and took him to the service.

Later that night, reflecting on his busy day, Gary told the story to other crusade volunteers.

"I would give anything if the people in my town were as dedicated and loved the Lord as much as that cripple," Gary said.

"They've always got excuses why they can't come to church in their air-conditioned cars with power brakes and power steering. They don't have as much

love for the Lord as that man: unwashed, unedu-
cated, and crawling on his hands and knees."

That kind of love and dedication lies at the heart
of the secret behind the thunder now building to a
roar in the Kyela District.

10
The Building Thunder

Thunder had rumbled throughout the afternoon, rolling down thousands of feet from the dark clouds formed against the vertical walls of the Livingstone Mountains.

Even in this semiquiescent state, the thunder echoed noisily in our valley between four sets of mountains: the Livingstones to the east of our farm, the Mporoto to the north, the Kipengere to the northeast, and the Undali to the west.

Now, in the deepening darkness, nature filled the valley with a truly awesome display of pyrotechnics as we tried to relax after a hard day's work. Brilliant but lethal lightning bolts flashed and sliced through the deluge of rain, and thunder reverberated deafeningly throughout the valley.

November was here: the early rains had arrived.

But the thunder had come first, building since early October about a month before the rains began. Initially, it was just a distant boom. As time passed, the volume gradually increased until the thunder was a deafening daily phenomenon.

As the thunderous crescendo had built, the valley

had eagerly awaited the first rains. Earth was parched from the dry spell which had gripped the area since August. Streams only trickled then, and the air was filled with dust and the smoke from brush fires Africans traditionally set to prepare the land for plowing.

Then, like a marvelous elixir of life, the rain broke in flooding torrents over the land and changed whole scenes in just a few days. Through the newly washed atmosphere we could see mountains more than a hundred miles away during the day. At night, the stars, free of their dingy filter, displayed themselves in a glory beyond anything we've seen anywhere else.

Mountain walls, parched and charred from the burning, changed like chameleons to shades ranging from chartreuse to deep blue-green, and a hundred unnamed falls spilled spectacularly from the Njombe plateau to the valley below. Birds sang with renewed vigor. Leaves burst from branches which had appeared dead. Flowers filled the fields, perfuming the air with nectar. Hues of bronze, magenta, red, and gold popped out everywhere.

Farmers plowed with yoked oxen. Fishermen cast their nets in vast, 360-mile-long Lake Nyasa to the south. Women tended garden plots and swayed under their burdens along bush roads. And the blood lily, a beautiful globe of red, sprang forth from its tuber hidden deep within the earth, signifying new life in the valley.

As the thunder crashed, and we prepared for sleep, we reflected on how much the thunder and

the coming of the rains reminded us of the coming
of Christianity to the Nyakyusa people here—from
the early days of embryonic Christian missions until
the present.

Long isolated by their geographical location, the
Nyakyusa had made little or no contact with the outside world before the mid-1800s.

Missionary-explorer-physician David Livingstone
passed this way and is credited by most as having
discovered Lake Nyasa in 1859, even though the
Africans knew about it all along. Other Europeans
followed.

Early German missionaries of the Berlin Mission
came up Lake Nyasa from the south to begin work in
what is now the Kyela District in the late 1800s.
Lutheran and Moravian missionaries followed in the
early 1900s, establishing three mission stations near
the lakeshore and, later, two in the mountains. In
time, other Lutheran and Moravian churches were
established in the area.

The presence of Lutheran and Moravian missionaries in our district has been sporadic since World
War II. Lutherans recently placed a missionary nurse
at Matema after a long period without any personnel
there.

Roman Catholics came into the area in 1936, establishing large churches at Ipinda village and Kyela
town. They now have a number of small congregations meeting under the guidance of trained national
catechists. Presently, two missionary priests of the
White Fathers reside at Ipinda, and one lives at
Kyela.

Other groups, represented to a limited extent in the district but without any mission personnel, include Pentecostals, Assemblies of God, Seventh-day Adventists, Church of God and Christ in Prophecy, Apostolic Church, and an indigenous sect called *Ngemela* or Last Church.

It's difficult to find reliable membership figures for these groups, but we estimate the Kyela District now has some fifty-thousand Lutherans and Moravians, five-thousand Catholics, and five thousand of the other groups.

That doesn't include statistics for either the Last Church sect or for Islam. The district has up to eight-hundred Muslims, but we have no way to estimate Last Church statistics accurately. Quite a few people list it as a preference when asked their church affiliation, but it doesn't appear to be very strong in the district.

Baptists, who began the 1980s with less than 3,800 members, had topped the 30,400-member mark as of mid-1986.

The thunder of the gospel was a faint, distant boom in the early, difficult days of missions when only a foothold was established. It has increased in decibels over the years, especially during the past two decades. The gospel message thundered forth, first from the inarticulate mouths of new missionaries. Then it reechoed from the throats of hundreds of Tanzanian pastors and guest preachers from abroad during our crusades.

It announced that God has come to cleanse people from sin with His Son, Christ Jesus, the Living Water.

Parched and dreary lives have revived, taking on new meaning and purpose. Dormant talents and gifts have sprung to life like flowers. People, dry and weary of sin, have been cleansed, refreshed, and restored in the increasing deluge of the wonderful message of God's love.

Sometimes we still can't believe how far things have come from the time in the mid-1960s when people here ran, thinking we'd come to shed their blood. The Africans themselves remember that with embarrassment.

In June, 1984, as we prepared to leave Tanzania for furlough, local pastors held a going-away party in our honor. They presented us with gifts, including a spear.

"Take this spear," they said, "to protect yourselves from the *wahuni* (hoodlums). We have heard on the radio that there is much crime in America."

I had to laugh. Twenty years earlier, the sight of a spear in our hands would have terrified them. Now some of the very men who had avoided us were arming us.

Gently kidding, we reminded them that once they feared we would draw their blood.

"Oh, Bwana Nepu," one pastor exclaimed with genuine remorse, "you must forget about that. That was before you brought the light of Jesus to us. Everyone in the district knows you're here because you love us and want to help us."

Back then, our name was synonymous with fear of the unknown; now it's synonymous with the local scene and, to many Africans, with white people in general.

Little children will often run along roads, pointing at unknown white passersby shouting, "Nepu, Nepu," instead of *"mzungu, mzungu."* In their minds, the travelers are white, so they must be "Nepus." Many Africans can't remember the time there hasn't been a "Nepu" here. As we noted earlier, we've lived in Tanzania longer than half of the Africans have been alive because of their short average life span and the high birth rate.

One little boy popped out of a banana grove to tell a lost volunteer from America how to find a bush church during our most recent crusade.

He pointed the way to what he called *"kanisa la Nepu"* ("Knapp's church"), and then disappeared as quickly as he'd appeared.

That kind of recognition is a mixed blessing. It's good to know the people accept us, but it's also extremely embarrassing when they say things like *"kanisa la Nepu."* We've emphasized over and over again—and will continue to emphasize—that the church belongs to God and His people, not to us. Fortunately, our maturing leaders in Kyela District churches don't make that mistake.

But we shouldn't take something like that too much to heart because we get enough doses of humility to offset it. For example, we took it as a compliment in the beginning when mothers held their little children aloft and pointed as we drove past. A compliment, we learned, hasn't always been the reason they did.

More than one parent has used us for the African
equivalent of: "If you don't be good, the 'boogie man'
will get you." They'll tell the children: "See those
wazungu? If you don't be good, we're going to send
you off with them."

That fate must certainly convince them to change
their ways!

Whatever Africans have thought of us over the
years, we're thankful God put us on a responsive
continent like Africa and in an unusually responsive
district like Kyela. Many missionaries aren't so
blessed.

Christianity is a new faith for most African believers who live on a continent where traditional reli-
gions, witchcraft, Islam, and other influences
compete for their hearts and minds. Over one third
of all African Christians are first-generation believers. It's much higher than that in the Kyela District.

But Christianity isn't new to the African continent
itself. It reached North Africa, Ethiopia, and Egypt
before reaching any of today's missionary-sending
nations of Europe and North America. The churches
of North Africa produced Christian giants such as
Tertullian, Origen, Cyprian, Clement, and Augus-
tine before they weakened and were swept away by
the onrush of Islam.

Missionary activity escalated dramatically during
the European rush for African colonies in the nine-
teenth century, and colonial-era missions led the way
in building schools and hospitals. But it wasn't until
the 1920s that Christianity began to make a real
dent, with a mass movement of people into the

church at a rate far more rapid than population growth. In fact, projections indicate much of Africa could be won to Christ in this century.

Despite wars, drought, difficult travel, economic distress, and backlash against foreign influences, the Christian population on the African continent is growing at nearly twice the rate of the general population. Church membership has surged from 8.8 million in 1900 to 115.9 million in 1970 to about 196.9 million in 1986 to a projected 323.9 million by the end of the century.

In 1900, after Southern Baptist missions had been in Africa for fifty years, we counted only six missionaries working with six churches, six preaching stations, and 385 believers. By the end of 1984, some 900 Southern Baptist missionaries worked in 32 African nations with more than 5,450 churches, nearly 3,450 preaching stations, and more than 758,000 believers.

Modern-day examples of people turning to Christ abound across Africa, even though we must be careful in determining what an African means when he says he's a "Christian." It can mean anything from a born-again believer to Christians who fall under other definitions, such as those who join for material gain, take a Christian name for cultural reasons, or experience infant baptism.

An African may well answer yes if you ask if he's a Christian, and then answer no if you follow up and ask if he's "saved," "born again," or if he has "accepted Jesus Christ as personal Savior."

Many other nuances affect African Christianity be-

cause just about any group you can name, from the
most peripheral sects to mainline liturgical denomi-
nations, has brought its version of Christianity to this
continent. For example, members of the *Ngemela* or
Last Church sect in our district sing Christian hymns
and often refer to themselves as Christian, but they
accept only the first five books of the Bible, baptize
in the name of Jacob, and practice polygamy. The
writings of their founder do not attest to the divinity
of Christ.

We deal with this and other problems in the Kyela
District, but the rewards make it worth the effort.
They have been considerable, with 33,775 total baptisms between 1978 and mid-1986 and growth across
the board.

Beginning with 1978, a time line of churches,
membership, baptisms, and contributions to churches numerically illustrates growth in the Kyela District:

(1) —60 congregations at the end of 1978 and 250
    at the end of 1985
(2) —3,740 church members at the end of 1978 and
    22,449 at the end of 1985
(3) —7,175 Tanzania shillings (about $422 US) in
    offerings from churches in 1978 and 323,336
    Tanzania shillings (about $19,020 US) in offer-
    ings in 1985
(4) —476 baptisms in the 1978 church year and
    7,973 in the 1985 church year.

Baptisms went up every year in the Kyela District
between the 1978 and 1985 church years, registering

escalating totals of 476; 504; 688; 1,786; 2,918; 5,339; 6,139; and 7,973.

Then we made a large surge forward. At this writing, with less than half the 1986 church year gone, the district had almost matched baptism totals for all of 1985 with 7,952 baptisms, mostly from the latest crusade. That raised our church membership to 30,401 at that point.

That kind of growth has attracted attention. In fact, a Baptist Press news service article once commented that our totals would lead the Southern Baptist Convention in annual baptisms if overseas statistics counted in the American tally.

That statement represents another one of those mixed blessings. It's good to get recognition, and we want growth like anyone else. But we don't want the impression created that we've done it alone. As we've indicated, Africans have played a primary role, and earlier missionaries, such as the DeBords and the Lewises, paved the way.

We don't want the impression created that chalking up numbers is the way to prove the authenticity of a particular ministry. Numbers are gratifying, but we know of too many cases where missionaries and pastors in difficult places at home and overseas work as hard as we do with much less to show for it, statistically.

That's even true in the "responsive" African scene we've described. Missionaries may work for years in certain places without many numbers. A lot of factors can cause that. It often happens, for example, in heavily Muslim areas.

Too many numbers-conscious people have forgotten that each person's job is to plan creatively and work hard under the leadership of the Holy Spirit and leave the results to His timing. High totals don't mean one person has a more valid ministry than another. The sower of spiritual seed may not always be the reaper, and the reaper may often gather what others have sown.

We've had the chance to do both over the years and have tried to analyze at least ten factors which have affected our sowing and reaping, along with an emphasis on prayer which has undergirded everything we do.

(1) *Longevity.* That, as we mentioned earlier, ranks as an important element in the category of factors. It takes time to gain people's confidence. We worked here sixteen years before we began to experience a real breakthrough.

(2) *Ministry of Assistance.* Closely related to longevity, our ministry of physical assistance has provided something people could appreciate and understand.

We started off in the early days trying to help them with their farming, going out and dealing in Christian love with problems they had on their farms in a practical, understandable way.

Even though our increasing emphasis on evangelism and church development has led to cutting back on the work of the farm, we've continued trying to improve ways of helping them over the years. For example, we provide such things as a land cultivation service, breeding animals, rabbits, hatching eggs, plants, and seeds.

We failed when we tried to help them launch a pineapple canning industry, although we improved the quality of local pineapples, now a regular part of their diet.

But as we observe their farms we can see many beneficial things we've helped introduce into our district such as cocoa, now an established cash crop and part of the economy, and improved poultry and livestock.

That's just part of the picture of how we've merged with their daily lives, but it illustrates the fact that they look on us as friends, not strangers. That goes a long way.

(3) *Special Concern for Pastors.* We've made an effort to help our pastors and be real friends to them. We would advise any missionary to major on the preachers and provide everything possible to help them develop the skills, confidence, and resources it takes to grow spiritually, win the lost, and develop their churches.

We have always tried to provide books, counsel, and training to help them develop spiritually and educationally, and we look for ways to help them meet their individual needs.

In other words, we try to treat each one as someone special, helping him find ways to take care of family problems, inviting him to tea and meals at our home, dropping other things to talk with him when he visits, and seeing to it he gets Bible training through home study, occasional seminars, or enroll-

ment at our pastors' training schools in the Rungwe
and Kyela Districts or at the Baptist seminary in Arusha.

Kyela District pastors have a feeling of comrade-
ship and teamwork in the task of evangelism and
church planting. That's an essential ingredient to
what has happened here. They'll do whatever they
can to please us because they know we care about
them, both as individuals and ministers of God.

Most of them have little or no education and labor
with little or no pay as bivocational farmer-pastors of
small bush churches. They need all the encouragement they can get.

(4) *Church Development Emphasis.* We put major
emphasis on church planting and encourage our pastors and their churches to start missions.

In earlier years, our work concentrated in villages
with no Christian witness, but since 1981 we've gone
on to establish a church in all the villages in the Kyela
District.

Multiplying the units—getting more and more
new churches going and getting a church within
walking distance of every person in the district—
gives us a framework for growth.

If you have only a few churches, and they're a long
distance away from a great many of the people, many
members can't attend faithfully. That's because they
live in a part of the world where they have no cars,
few buses, and not very many working bicycles.

People here need a church right there, nearby,
and that dovetails with our master plan. A lot of small
churches, located close to the people and spaced

closely together, have spurred growth. Missionaries Harold and Betty Cummins, who have started many churches in Kenya, agree with that approach. They advocate locating bush churches not more than two or three miles apart.

(5) *Use of National Evangelists.* This group of six African men, which recently grew to eight, lies at the heart of our plan for church planting and development. As pastors, they had developed a number of strong churches and missions on their own when it occurred to us to recruit them as the centerpiece of our plan.

We found the resources to provide each one a motorcycle so he could fan out over his own assigned subdivision of the district to preach, start churches, recruit and train pastors, and help our pastors, youth leaders, and women's leaders train people throughout the district.

The evangelists, whom we expect eventually to work themselves out of a job, began work with the goal of launching a church in every village in their area. Now that they've done that, they're concentrating on working with inexperienced pastors of new, weak little churches to help them develop effective ministries.

We couldn't have done this in our first year here, or even in the tenth, because we had to develop some men who were mature, had proven themselves as preachers and church planters, and had reached the point where they had enough experience to help someone else.

(6) *Youth and Women's Programs.* We've already

outlined Evelyn's work in launching the youth program which has played a major role in our evangelism and church development. She has also devoted a lot of attention to developing women's work. We have seventeen African youth leaders and six African women's leaders assisting throughout the district.

(7) *Regular Evangelistic Campaigns.* As we've mentioned, regular crusades since 1976 have produced amazing results. They keep Christians enthusiastic and reach the lost. All the other things we do to create a favorable environment wouldn't pay off unless we got out there and confronted people with the claims of Christ on their lives and reaped the harvest from all the seeds we'd planted.

That increasing harvest has created a pressing, growing need for follow-up. We've used new-member classes taught by ourselves, the African evangelists, the better-trained pastors, or others brought in from the outside. But the task escalates, and so much more could be done. We can use all the help we can get to keep the follow-up on track.

Some have asked if all the numbers reported out of the Kyela District represent real depth. That's a good question because numbers without depth will blow away with the wind.

Clell Coleman, associate pastor of Sheridan Hills Baptist Church in Hollywood, Florida, gave an unsolicited testimonial to the depth of our work in a recent conversation with a friend in the States.

"I'd heard about all the numbers in the Kyela District and went out there wondering if there was real depth," said Clell, one of the volunteers in the record-breaking crusade in late 1985.

"I discovered the Knapps' ministry has permeated the whole thousand-square-mile district—both on the surface and on a much deeper level.

"From a surface point of view, you hear the children shouting, 'Nepu, Nepu' as you drive through the district," Clell continued. "On a deeper level, you meet people everywhere you go who've had the Knapps bury their dead, visit their sick, give them food, medicine, clothing or books, counsel them with their problems, preach the gospel to them, and teach them how to grow spiritually."

Clell said he marveled at the ability of Africans in the district to understand the gospel, perceive spiritual things, and ask questions.

"As they wrestled with a decision to accept Christ, they asked me questions about life, death, sin, God, salvation, heaven, and hell, which showed they had really been exposed to who God is and had thought deeply about what He means to them," Clell said.

"I came away feeling these decisions aren't just a pile of numbers but represent people who have really committed their lives to Christ and will make an impact on Africa."

Clell's son, Mark, who also accompanied the team as one of the crusade volunteers, came away with the conviction that he'll return to Africa as a missionary after finishing college and seminary.

We appreciate Clell's observations because we've felt that our church-centered approach and steady pattern of growth indicate we've successfully prepared the district for evangelization and conserved the harvest to this point.

But it's a never-ending job. We don't think our ministry will continue to prosper without more missionaries to teach and equip, as we'll discuss later.

(8) *Use of Volunteers.* The crusades also have made good use of volunteers, such as Clell Coleman and others from America, who draw crowds in the Kyela District. They make a big impact on our churches, then they return to the United States to reenergize their own churches toward more missions involvement. In fact, volunteers from America have made a big impact on Southern Baptist missions in general.

In 1984, nearly sixty-one-hundred long- and short-term volunteers, almost 30 percent more than in 1983, served in 45 countries and helped lead more than seventeen-thousand people to faith in Christ. The Foreign Mission Board expects to reach a goal of sending ten-thousand volunteers overseas every year by the end of the century.

The success of the volunteers demonstrates how much power Southern Baptists have in the pew and what an effective job committed laypersons can do. Volunteers, both pastor and laity, have played a big part in our evangelism, efforts to follow up our crusade results, and ongoing programs of church construction.

(9) *Church Construction.* From the early days, even when Bill Lewis was here, efforts have been made to help the stronger churches put up a permanent building which would last for many years.

Church members make the bricks and provide labor. We help with the sheet iron for the roof, the hardware for the building, and some skilled labor. A building can cost at least ten-thousand dollars.

In the late 1970s, we went for five years without any construction funds available during a high period of growth. That left our churches in desperate need for more and better buildings.

A real breakthrough came during the 1982 crusade when volunteers saw the needs and found ways to help, including sending Mark Kissee, a licensed contractor, and his wife, Cathy, out for a two-year term as volunteers to supervise church construction. They came from the Sheridan Hills Church in Hollywood, Florida.

A number of groups, individuals, and churches have assisted at this point over the years as well as in other areas of need. We dare not try to list names because we could leave important ones out, but the Kissees, who gave two years of their lives to live and work in the Kyela District, played an indispensable role. They're now aiming for a career in missions.

(10) *Emphasis on Schools.* As long as we don't try to force anyone to be Baptist, most of the public schools in the Kyela District are wide open to us for preaching and teaching. In fact, 9,525 of the professions of faith in the latest crusade—over 75 percent—came from the schools, one of the focal points of our strategy.

Foreign missionaries are nearly always optimists, seeing their work in terms of their hopes and dreams, discounting or overlooking negative developments, and emphasizing and glorying in the hopeful signs they see, no matter how small. Like the farmer who plants the seed, they visualize a mature crop and an abundant harvest despite the pitfalls and disappointments.

We're as likely to fall into that pattern as any other missionaries, but we still believe growth in the Kyela District will be even more exciting in the future. For example, we believe it's not too radical to project that our membership will grow from 30,401 in mid-1986 to more than 100,000, maybe 150,000, by 1995.

Kyela has added 190 new congregations since 1978 to saturate the area. So it's not likely we'll add many more new churches. However, our average congregation has only about 125 members. Since some of our largest churches have 500 to 800 members, there's plenty of room for growth in existing churches. Membership grew sixfold in the eight-year period 1978 through 1985. Another eight years of that kind of growth could give the district nearly 135,000 by 1993 alone.

But the calendar and the frailty of the flesh tell us something that hopes and dreams can't blur into unreality, no matter how much we readjust our rose-colored glasses.

Let's be candid. In 1993, if something like "Land Rover neck" doesn't get us first, I will be sixty-six years old, and Evelyn will be sixty-three. Considering the rigors of life in this area, we should be retired before then.

Who will pick up the work here to keep it developing until enough pastors and national leaders can be trained to carry on?

Frankly, some observers, noting that we've had such a highly individualistic approach to missions here over the years, have wondered if successors could fit effectively into the Kyela District mold.

But we can't believe that when God's Spirit is moving, He won't raise up others who can carry on. We're praying—and urge others to pray—that God will do so.

We sincerely believe the movement here in Kyela, at this critical stage of its development, won't last and won't reach its potential growth without additional missionary personnel.

Our greatest need is training and equipping pastors as part of the overall strategy for conserving the results of the crusades of the past and those to come. Trained pastors are the key to developing mature Christians and strong churches.

Sustained growth will depend in the long run on the skills, accomplishments, and commitment of our African leaders. There was a day when we could assemble all the Kyela pastors in our large living room. Today, with 250 pastors, there's no way to do that—or even know them all very well.[1]

Kyela District must have additional missionary personnel to work at least through the final years of the twentieth century and concentrate heavily on training and equipping these men and others throughout the area.

Missions history contains many examples of situations where rapid church growth has turned into a rapid falling away or a move toward heresy without proper nurturing by adequate missionary personnel.

Of course, there are exceptions to that, but we believe that, basically, missionary personnel are the
key.

We've struggled too hard to develop adequate follow-up on new converts in the district to want to see
the nurturing phase begin to fade in the years following our eventual departure.

But there's an even larger perspective to consider.
When we get back to our dreams for the future, the
need for continued stability takes on greater signifi-
cance than just what can happen in Kyela. We see
the district as a power center for evangelistic advance throughout the country, and into surrounding
countries.

History shows a pattern of great missions move-
ments coming from a strong, enthusiastic center
where a community of praying Christians has actually experienced the gospel in their own lives and has
seen what can happen under the leadership of the
Holy Spirit. You see it from the New Testament days
of the great church in Jerusalem, to the beginning of
the modern missions movement in England, to current missions efforts which flow out to the whole
world from the power center of the so-called "Bible
Belt" in America.

Kyela can be this kind of powerhouse for carrying
the gospel to all of Tanzania and neighboring countries because we've got a going thing here with many
churches and many people who have seen how the
gospel can spread.

We have responsive people who expect others to

be responsive and who find opportunities to share their faith.

And we're a district of travelers. Kyela is overcrowded, and every year thousands move away, not just to other parts of Tanzania but to all parts of central and southern Africa to find new economic opportunities. That includes many of our members. We can cite a number of specific incidences where our members have started churches or even whole associations of churches because they carried the gospel with them.

Our team of eight African evangelists has begun doing the same thing in unevangelized areas surrounding Kyela.

And we've already told how one of the evangelists, Simoni Mwambobe, carried the gospel across the Songwe River into Malawi and may well qualify as Tanzania Baptists' first "foreign missionary."

But the greatest force for the future lies in the corps of young people which grew out of Evelyn's work with youth when we learned a lesson about God's arithmetic.

Our reservoir, now twenty-five-hundred persons strong, includes young people bursting with a zeal for God's work and equipped with many more advantages than older pastors and leaders in most of our existing churches in the Kyela District.

They have more formal education. They grew up in the church, while the older generation found Christ later in life. They have many Bible skills their elders lack, most having gone through our Scripture-

memorization, Bible-drill, and public-speaking training.

Some have had leadership roles in our Bible club
program, and some have gone on to complete our
pastors' training schools and become pastors. These
young people have a potential which can truly un-
leash the building thunder of the gospel in our country, but most haven't yet found an opportunity for
leadership outside the youth program.

When we think of them, we think of what one
writer commented about potential. It fits everything
we've said about the building thunder. "We journey
together between the lightning and the thunder," he
wrote in *At the Crossroads,* a publication of the Communications Era Task Force.

"We journey between the flash of recognition of
what is happening to us and the reverberations of
what we are willing to do about it."[2]

Our flash of recognition at what our young people
can do took place recently. Now it's up to us and
other missionaries to face the reverberations of what
we're willing to do to tap their potential, as well as
the potential of many Kyela District residents moving to other areas.

Charles and Betty Bedenbaugh, missionaries in the
extremely hard-to-crack, heavily-Muslim Tanga area
along the coast of Tanzania, have already done something about it. Growth had been extremely slow
there over the past twenty years as several missionaries worked hard but ran into a brick wall in an
environment which has had centuries of Arab influence.

We discussed the situation with the Bedenbaughs at our 1983 mission meeting as they girded up to take a crack at their new assignment in Tanga. Our discussion produced a brainstorm. Why not send a team of nationals from the Kyela District to work with the Bedenbaughs?

A five-man team, made up of two mature pastors and three young men who had come up through our youth program, went to Tanga for eight months to do just that. Each was to start a church in one of the villages and train a man to assume the pastorate.

Eight months later they returned home, bursting with excitement about what had happened. They left behind five churches and two preaching points in villages where no previous Christian witness had existed, fifty-eight baptized believers and a number of others awaiting baptism.

Two of the churches invited two of the younger men to return to work with them over a two-year period. One of these men has been elected chairman of the newly formed Tanga Baptist Association. That's just an inkling of how the reservoir of youth can provide the resources for great strides in home missions in Tanzania.

Fifty-eight baptisms may not sound impressive compared to other statistics, but for the Tanga region it represents a great leap forward.

We hope other teams will go out from Kyela to various points in Tanzania where they can establish new work, with special emphasis on areas where our members have migrated. We've left no doubt about our view of the importance of the career missionary in all of this, but dedicated African preachers have set a pattern in Tanzania which challenges us all.

Missionaries work in a number of areas in Tanzania today which Africans opened up for them—from the time Anosisye Mwangwembe came through the mist for Sammy DeBord to the present. Who can forget or fail to be inspired by that kind of example?

Wherever people live on this great continent, the land is coursed with a multitude of tiny, intertwining footpaths.

In the Kyela District, these byways enter every nook and cranny of the district, climb the surrounding mountains, and encircle the great lake to the south.

Some have postulated that one could follow these paths to every part of Africa where people live. Here in Kyela, they have provided the thoroughfare for taking the gospel to every village in the district and beyond.

Primarily, it's the national pastors and evangelists who have trod—or in a few cases ridden—over these paths to remote and isolated settlements to find people who need to know that the Savior has come. They've crossed rivers, braved snakes and crocodiles, and climbed the surrounding mountains to take the message to neighboring tribes.

As we look down these paths toward Tanzania's spiritual future, trying to see what will happen next, what do we see out ahead?

Bloodstained footprints in the dust?

Yes. They're the footprints of the old African man named Andelile, who climbed mountains barefooted to tell others about Jesus Christ. They're the footprints of so many others whose bare feet have been torn by thorns and cut by rocks.

Like Andelile, men such as Anosisye, Simoni, Johnstoni, Ayubu, and a host of others, have literally sown the path with drops of their own blood to preach Christ with thundering messages of repentance and salvation.

We must follow these blood-sprinkled paths faithfully, sacrificially, and repeatedly if we expect the building thunder to rock this nation—and this whole continent—for Jesus Christ.

Notes

1. The day will come, in the development of truly indigenous work, for missionaries to move on to something else and leave it in the hands of Africans in the district. But much remains to be done before then.

2. From *At the Crossroads*, a publication of the Communications Era Task Force. Box 3623, Spokane, WA 99220 U.S.A. © 1983, 1984 Communications Era Task Force.

Epilogue:
That Magnificent Obsession

By Robert O'Brien

An African proverb says that once you've drunk the water of Africa you'll always return.

I did. I returned—not only to visit—but to live with my family and travel there for more than two years on assignment from the Foreign Mission Board. We went there to field test the idea of locating four regional writer-missionaries at key points around the world to live in the scene and report the true heartbeat of Southern Baptist missions.

That intensive experience revolutionized my understanding of missions and changed forever the way I'll write about it. It began moving my missions understanding from the *sidewalk* to the *subway*—terms Kenya missionary Dan Schellenberg uses to describe the difference between the surface and the depth. Of course, true "subway" knowledge and insight develop only after longtime experience on the scene—and, frankly, more with some individuals than others, regardless of tenure.

When our regional writer-missionaries finally arrive in their various locations and begin to explore the subway, what will they find?

They'll find what I did—missionaries and national Christians working in difficult circumstances amidst a staggering variety of spiritual and physical needs. They'll find that those missionaries don't wear halos or live in angelic isolation from their humanity.

In fact, they're very human. That should not disturb Southern Baptists, the all-too-human body of believers from whence they come.

So our missionary writers—experienced chroniclers of the Southern Baptist scene at home—probably won't marvel too much at what God has accomplished overseas, despite our humanity. They'll already have experienced that phenomenon in America.

They won't marvel at the fact that different missionaries have different roles, styles, personalities, attitudes, abilities, results, and philosophies—and that they don't always agree with each other about how things should be done.

Why should they?

Hasn't that been common among Christians down through church history, as well as in Southern Baptist life at home? And doesn't each member of the Body of Christ have different functions and gifts to complement the whole at home and abroad?

But we all should marvel at that intensely burning sense of divine calling—indeed, that magnificent obsession—which causes missionaries to persevere in distant Third World lands and keep chipping away at obstacles which most people in developed America would find unbearable. Why else would a couple like Doug and Evelyn Knapp, main characters in *Thun-*

der in the Valley, plant their lives for more than two decades in some of Africa's most remote bush country?

The idea of writing *Thunder in the Valley* wasn't even a distant rumble in our brains when Doug, Evelyn, and I first met in 1982, not long after I arrived in Africa with my wife, Shirley, and our two sons, Eric and Paul. But before long, as I talked to them and visited their work during my travels in twenty countries of Africa, it became obvious the Knapps had a story to tell.

Deep in a valley in Tanzania's remote Kyela (Key-AY-lah) District, thousands of people were turning to Jesus Christ in a ministry which had escalated over two decades under their patient nurturing.

Their story had been told before, but not in the detail it needed to reflect the true depth of the spiritual breakthroughs which have resulted in nearly thirty-four thousand baptisms in Kyela between 1978 and mid-1986.

A series of articles in various denominational publications attracted a lot of attention and played a large part in setting up, in 1984-85, the busiest furlough year that the Knapps have ever had.

After a hectic speaking schedule all across the country, Doug quipped that he'd be glad to get back to the mission field where he could slow down to a run.

Still, we didn't think in terms of a book.

But Owen Cooper of Yazoo City, Mississippi, did. Cooper, denominational statesman and layperson par excellence, began gathering what proved to be valuable data for such an effort and approached Broadman Press with the idea. Broadman picked up on it, one thing led to another, and eventually *Thunder in the Valley* was rumbling. The Knapps and I would collaborate on the manuscript and Cooper would write the foreword.

The Knapps and I got together once in Florida before they returned to Tanzania from furlough and later on a follow-up trip I took to Tanzania. But our collaboration was basically long-distance. Versions of the manuscript went back and forth, and the Knapps traveled hours on bush roads to get to a telephone for conferences. They have no phone on their remote mission station in Makwale (Mah-KWAH-lay).

One such exchange boggled the mind of our long-suffering editor at Broadman, who had waited through our protracted intercontinental gyrations with growing anticipation for some sign that a manuscript actually existed.

As the deadline bore down on us like vultures circling over a wounded eland in the African bush, the manuscript journeyed by special courier to Nairobi, Kenya. There, missionaries put it on a small Missionary Aviation Fellowship plane to distant Dodoma, Tanzania. From there, another small mission plane ferried it on to Mbeya to await the Knapps, who traveled overland in a four-wheel-drive vehicle to pick it up, study it, and telephone me in the United States.

"Goodness gracious! With our luck, a lion's likely to jump up out of the bush and eat the manuscript," our editor quipped. But the lions had to make do with

other prey. Somehow, we dodged all the mishaps
which could have derailed our hazardous "mail" service, finished our transoceanic collaboration, and
sent the finished product to Nashville, Tennessee.

The process produced some tensions and pressures
but generated some new insights. One such insightful moment came at the Bahari Beach Hotel in Dar
es Salaam, Tanzania, as I watched Doug let the sun
and surf soothe the pains of "Land Rover neck,"
mentioned in Chapter 9.

He and Evelyn had just finished an intensive period of work in Makwale, in cooperation with volunteers from Florida, which had resulted in more than
12,600 professions of faith.

The moment of relaxation would be only fleeting
as they prepared to return to Makwale for the follow-
up phase of the crusade. Anything similar to "Land
Rover neck" would cause many Americans to stay
home from desks jobs in air-conditioned offices.
Doug was getting ready to go back to the bush and
its devastating roads.

I knew what he faced because I was going through
a case of what you could call "Land Rover back." My
sacroiliac strain, or whatever it was, had begun with
a fall, on an earlier trip to the Ethiopian highlands to
cover the hunger relief efforts. It had apparently
healed, but that didn't take Tanzania's roads into
consideration. The rough roads to Makwale had rein-
jured it on the first day out there, and I'd limped
painfully for the entire trip, determined to finish
before returning home to get proper treatment.

But Doug (and Evelyn, who has had recurring back

problems over the years) would need more determination than that. They had just returned to Tanzania from furlough and would keep plugging away for the rest of their term of service, over bush roads and under bush conditions.

Like most missionaries and others who have their eyes fixed on a divine goal, they let very little get in their way. If they can't go around obstacles they go through them, such as the menacing group of pagan witchdoctors they faced recently in the Kalahari Desert about fifteen miles out of Gaborone, capital of the African nation of Botswana.

The Knapps had traveled there to view the passing of Halley's Comet. Experts had listed the Kalahari Desert in western Botswana as one of the ten best places in the world to view the comet. The Knapps and Botswana Missionary Fern Dannelly of Michigan had found the perfect spot, they thought. They parked their car and climbed up onto an outcropping of rocks for a once-in-a-lifetime view of the comet.

But events on the ground made a greater impression than the disappointing comet, which looked like a distant, fuzzy cotton ball, even under the best desert viewing conditions.

After a few minutes, several African witchdoctors arrived, brandishing spears, long animal horns, and fly whisks (made from the hairy tips of cows' tails attached to ornate wooden handles). One thrust a long horn into the ground in front of the car and fell down near it, uttering incantations. The others surrounded the three missionaries, intimidating them with their fly whisks, spears, and menacing cries.

The missionaries, uneasy but determined, walked straight toward the witchdoctors, praying aloud for God's protection. None of the gyrating, threatening men touched them as they climbed down from the rocks, made their way slowly to the car, got in, and drove away.

They left a surprised group of witchdoctors standing in their dust.

No one back home in Tanzania's thousand-square-mile Kyela District would have been surprised. They've worked with the *Nepus* (Knapps) too long to be surprised at the power of their faith or at their tenacity—or at their single-minded determination to fulfill their magnificent obsession of winning the district to Jesus Christ.

Like the title of the famous novel by Lloyd C. Douglas about a person obsessed with giving himself in the service of others, their magnificent obsession stands out as a common thread in the work of missionaries around the world. It should cause each of us, wherever we are, to pause and determine if our own obsession is magnificent enough to push us as powerfully forward in service to God.

Glossary

Glossary for translation and pronunciation of words used in the Swahili language, unless otherwise identified

A

Asante sana (Ah-*SAHN*-teh *SAH*-nah)—"Thank you very much."
ayah (*AH*-yah)—A child's nurse, baby-sitter

B

bega kwa bega (*BAY*-gah kwah BAY-gah)—shoulder to shoulder
bwana (*BWAH*-nah)—mister, master

C

chai (*CHAH*-ee)—tea
choo (choh)—toilet

D

daraja (dah-*RAH*-jah)—bridge
Daraja la Mungu (Dah-*RAH*-jah lah *MOON*-ngoo)— God's Bridge, a natural bridge in Tanzania.

dawa (*DAH*-wah)—medicine
duka (*DOO*-kah)—a small shop or store

F

fundi (*FOON*-dee)—expert

H

Haba na haba hujaza kibaba (*HAH*-bah nah *HAH*-bah hoo-*JAH*-zah kee-*BAH*-bah)—"Drop by drop the bucket fills." A Swahili proverb.
Hodi? (*HOH*-dee?)—"May I come in?"
Hujambo, habari, Bwana? (Hoo-JAHM-boh, hah-BAH-ree, BWAH-nah?)—"Hello, how are things, mister?"

J

jitihada (jee-tee-*HAH*-dah)—crusade

K

kanga (*KAHNG*-gah)—Cloth women wrap as garments around their bodies and their head.
kanisa (kah-*NEE*-sah)—church
kanisa la Kibatisti (kah-*NEE*-sah lah Kee-bah-*TEES*-tee)—Baptist church
Karibu (Kah-*REE*-boo)—"Come in, draw near." A greeting which varies in usage but is usually given as an invitation to enter a home after a visitor says, "Hodi?" ("May I come in?")
Kristo (*KREES*-toh)—Christ
kuku (*KOO*-koo)—chicken, hen
kwa heri (kwah *HEH*-ree)—goodbye

Kyala (Kee-*AH*-lah)—Word in the language of the *Nyakyusa* (N-nyah-*KYOO*-sah) tribe for the one Creator God

Kyela (Key-AY-lah)—Name of the one-thousand-square-mile district in Southwestern Tanzania where the Knapps work.

M

mahindi (mah-*HEEN*-dee)—corn

maji (*MAH*-jee)—water

makofi (mah-*KOH*-fee)—palms of the hand

Makwale (Mah-*KWAH*-lay)—town in Tanzania's Kyela District where the Knapps live.

mama (*MAH*-mah)—mother or frequent term of address for women

matatu (mah-*TAH*-too)—Term for the covered pick-up-truck-type vehicle used as a low-cost taxi for Africans.

Mau Mau (*MAH*-oo *MAH*-oo)—Name given to militants of the Kikuyu tribe in Kenya, who advocated terrorism and violent opposition to British rule in the early to mid 1950s. The name is also associated with ritual oaths Mau Mau leaders enforced to promote loyalty within the the independence movement.

mayai (mah-*YAH*-ee)—eggs

maziwa (mah-*ZEE*-wah)—milk

mbegu (m-m*BEH*-goo)—seed(s)

mchawi (m-m*CHA*-wee)—witch doctor

mchumba (m-m*CHOOM*-bah)—fiancée

moran (*MOH*-rahn)—Masai warrior

mtihani (m-mtee-*HAH*-nee)—scholastic test or examination

mtoto (m-m*TOH*-toh)—child (plural, *watoto*)

muhogo (moo-*HOH*-goh)—cooked casava roots

Mungu (*MOON*-ngoo)—God

mzee (m-m*ZAY*-ay)—respected elder leader (plural, *wazee*)

mzungu (m-m*ZOON*-ngoo)—white person (plural, *wazungu*)

N

Nataka maji (Nah-*TAH*-kah *MAH*-jee)—"I want some water."

ndio (n-n*DEE*-oh)—yes

ndugu (n-n*DOO*-goo)—brother

Nepu (*NEH*-poo)—Pronunciation for Doug and Evelyn Knapp's last name in Tanzania's Kyela District

Nglonda ulukama (N-ngah-*LOHN*-dah oo-loo-*KAH*-mah)—Words in the language of the *Nyakyusa* (N-nyah-*KYOO*-sah) tribe for "I want some milk."

Ngemela (N-ngay-*MAY*-lah)—Last Church sect

ng'ombe (n-n-g [silent n-g]-*OHM*-bay)—cow(s)

Nyakyusa (N-nyah-*KYOO*-sah)—African tribe the Knapps work with in Tanzania's Kyela District

nyuki (n-n*YOO*-kee)—bee(s)

P

pole (*POH*-lay)—a term of condolence

pori (*POH*-ree)—wild country

Piga makofi matatu (*PEE*-gah mah-*KOH*-fee mah-

TAH-too)—"Strike three palms" or clap three times.

S

safari (sah-*FAH*-ree)—trip or journey

samosa (sah-*MOH*-sah)—Asian (Indian) hand food made from meat and onions deep fried in flour pastry.

sauti (sah-*OO*-tee)—voice

Sauti ya Wabatisti (Sah-*OO*-tee yah Wah-bah-*TEES*-tee)—*The Baptist Voice*, publication of the Kyela Baptist Association.

shamba (*SHAHM*-bah)—farm or garden

Shetani (Shay-*TAH*-nee)—Satan

Sijambo (See-*JAHM*-boh)—"I'm all right, thanks."

U

ugali—(oo-*GAH*-lee)—An African staple dish made from boiled, ground corn.

Usetani (Oo-say-*TAH*-nee)—Word in the language of the *Nyakyusa* (N-nyah-*KYOO*-sah) tribe for Satan.

V

vigelegele (vee-gay-lay-*GAY*-lay)—high-pitched warbling trill ("ululating") women give as a sign of approval.

W

Wabatisti (Wah-bah-*TEES*-tee)—Baptists; Baptist people.

wahuni (wah-*HOO*-nee)—hoodlums

watoto (wah-*TOH*-toh)—children (singular, *mtoto*)

wazee (wah-*ZAY*-ay)—respected elder leaders (singular, *mzee*)

wazungu (wah-*ZOON*-ngoo)—white people (singular, *mzungu*)